What Bob's peers say:

Bob 'Idea Man' Hooey is a master of public speaking, not only in Canada, but internationally. Not only has he motivated, inspired, and energized tens of thousands of people in his audiences worldwide, he also takes the time to work with aspiring and developing speakers to help them hone their skills and perfect their craft so they can be their very best on the platform and in the business.

If you are interested in public speaking, or you are developing a career as a professional speaker, trainer or keynoter, Bob's wisdom will help you get there.
Sarah Elaine Eaton, Ph.D., CAPS professional member

If your company needs new and creative ideas, I highly recommend Canada's Ideaman, Bob Hooey. He has sincere passion for helping others to succeed and guiding them to reach their highest potential. You are leaving a legacy. Thank you.
Debra Kasowski, CAPS professional member

Good news is always good! Congratulations on this wonderful achievement - well deserved, I'm sure! And how gracious of you to "share" this award with so many others - you're a true leader and a real gentleman! **Chris Ford**, DTM, Past International President (2007-2008) Toastmasters International

Congratulations on the Spirit of CAPS Award. You have worked long and hard on behalf of CAPS…helped many speakers including me and richly deserve this award. Well done my friend. **Peter Legge**, CSP, Hof, CPAE

Congratulations on winning the Spirit of CAPS award. I can think of no one who more richly deserved the award. Your acceptance speech moved us all of reminding us what's it's all about. Your humility and graciousness was inspiring. Congratulations again my friend.
Michael Bayer, CSP, 2012 President CAPS Winnipeg

Bob 'Idea Man' Hooey is a mentor to many and has done great things for CAPS Edmonton. Bob has also provided me with innovative ideas to help grow my business. His commitment to CAPS, the speaking profession, and professional speakers is admirable! It is a pleasure to recommend Bob. **Charmaine Hammond**, Hammond International Inc., Past Director CAPS Edmonton

i

Bob 'Idea Man' Hooey is an exceptional speaker and facilitator who helps businesses and organizations grow profit and create effective teams. This leadership and sales expert has written nearly a dozen books, travels the globe speaking to managers, corporations, and non-profits, increasing morale as well as profits. Bob is a leader within the speaking industry and is beloved by his peers for his mentorship, warmth and high skill. I highly recommend Bob as a speaker. He'll be the one your employees and conference attendees talk about. **Shawne Duperon**, CEO, ShawneTV (3-time Emmy award winner)

I have known Bob Hooey for many years through the Canadian Association of Professional Speakers organization. He has been an inspiration to our members and has received international recognition. I guarantee that when you work with Bob you will never be disappointed. **Vera Goodman**, President, Reading Wings, CAPS member

I had the pleasure of hearing and watching Bob Hooey deliver a keynote speech several years ago when he gave a presentation at a Toastmasters International Convention. Bob impressed me greatly with his professionalism, energy, and ability to connect with his audience while giving them value. I heartily recommend this talented speaker and "Idea Farmer" to all who want to move to the next level. **Dilip Abayasekara**, DTM, Accredited Speaker, Past International President, Toastmasters International

Top qualities: *Personable, Expert, and Creative. Bob Hooey's ability to engage audiences combined with his insightfulness and humor, render him an outstanding and dynamic presenter. He combines a high level of energy and creativity to his sessions which is coupled with his keen business and leadership sense. His unwavering commitment to mutually beneficial business relationships makes Bob a trusted colleague, mentor, and professional asset to those individuals or organizations who choose to work with him.* **Michelle Devlin**, DTM, 2012 Director CAPS Edmonton

Bob has coached the Senior Executive members of the District 42 Toastmasters for several years, serving as a Trainer & Mentor at our annual experiential training event. In addition to sharing his knowledge and experience with the leaders in our organization, he has been very helpful & influential to me personally. Bob is worth every penny of your investment in his services... and then some! But let's not tell him that!! **Troy Wruck**, DTM, Past District 42 Governor, Toastmasters International

Just wanted to tell you how meaningful your session and materials were to me. I must say that it helped me considerably in so many ways that have practical application immediately. I'm so grateful to you for creating awareness and understanding of how to improve myself as a professional speaker. **Nancy Kindler**, Past CAPS Edmonton President

Speaks from his heart, uses humor and stories to bring his theory and concepts alive. **Linda Maul**, Creating People Power, Past President CAPS Edmonton

7th Edition

Speaking
for $uccess

Adding mastery to your message and power to your presentation!

Bob 'Idea Man' Hooey

Accredited Speaker

2011 Spirit of CAPS recipient

Success Publications

*Dedicated to my wife, Irene, whose encouragement
and dedicated support inspires me to continue*
Speaking for Success!

*Dedicated as well to those speakers whose
encouragement and example have helped
me hone the skills needed to continue*
Speaking for Success!

13 steps, a shaky start

The night was dark, it was raining, and the wind was howling. There were 13 steps, in a darkened outside entrance from the dimly lit parking lot, down into the basement meeting room. How did I know? I counted them as I went down, went back up, and, then, *screwed up* my courage and went back down again.

I descended slowly, hesitantly for the second time, reached out and nervously placed my hand on the door knob. My heart was pumping (fast ☺), my legs were shaky, and my breathing was short and labored. Was I making the right decision? What would I find on the other side of the door? Maybe I should just turn around and go home? How would I react? Would they like me, help me, or reject me? *"Ok, Hooey, go for it!"*

I put a *forced* smile on my face, turned the knob, and opened the door. I stood there for a minute, took a deep breath, and stepped into **Toastmasters of Today! I made that first step that has taken me around the world sharing my message of hope.**

I still remember my first visit that Tuesday night in April 1991. I was *nervous* and shy. Now, anyone who knows me will find that hard to believe, but it was very true, then. This was a scary moment for me. I had just come through a devastating and debilitating divorce. Frankly, I didn't feel very confident in myself or my abilities. If you're a Toastmaster, remember your first visit to your club. Perhaps, like me, you felt a little nervous or intimidated by members who could get up and seemingly speak without notes or nervousness.

I was there, reviving a dream of being a professional speaker and someday being able to stand on the big stage sharing my ideas, travelling the world, and inspiring and investing in the lives of those in the audience.

What I found at the bottom of those 13 steps was a supportive, friendly group of people who befriended me and became my champions, coaches, and cheerleaders; some of whom still play that role today.

1

- Perhaps you have had a similar experience as you began something?
- Perhaps you are feeling a bit shaky about starting down this path to being a better speaker?
- Perhaps you have played a similar role in the growth of a Toastmaster member or business friend?

That **one step** into the room, following the 13 down made an amazing difference in my life and my career. ***Update 2012:*** *I have now been a professional speaker for over 16 years and have been to 35 countries on 4 continents, so far.*

In 1998, I had the *distinct* pleasure of walking across a Palm Desert, California stage to be inducted into the Toastmasters International Hall of Fame as the 48th professional level Accredited Speaker in our history.

In 2008, I had the *rare* privilege of keynoting the leadership luncheon at the Toastmasters International convention. As part of my introduction they played the video of me walking across that Palm Desert stage. My first words were, **"*I may have walked across that stage by myself… but I did not get there by myself!*"**

- It took those first 13 steps, ***plus*** the loving, supportive investment of thousands of fellow Toastmasters, CAPS, GSF, and NSA colleagues, over many years, to help move me toward that goal.
- It took those first 13 steps to start me on the path to living my dream of travelling the world sharing ideas and challenging people to reach out and build foundations of success under their dreams.

Last year (2011) I was selected as one of 300 Toastmasters International Ambassadors around the globe appointed as influencers to help with the launch of the first re-brand in their history. I was glad to serve and give back to this amazing organization.

When I received **The Spirit of CAPS** award (the highest award given in our Canadian speaking industry) at our 2011 Canadian Association of Professional Speakers convention in Toronto, I shared it with those in attendance. I emphasized that all the nice things our President Ravi Tangri, CSP mentioned in his introduction were not accomplished, *"by myself"*. I simply asked for help, a lot, and got it. So can you!

Your dream may not be to become a professional speaker. But, if you have invested in this book my guess is you have a desire to become a better, more confident speaker, right? What follows in these **Speaking for Success** pages are tips, creative techniques, proven ideas, and exercises to help you move that dream or desire into a reality.

What is your next step?

Bob 'Idea Man' Hooey
Distinguished Toastmaster
Past District 21 Governor
Accredited Speaker
2011 Spirit of CAPS recipient
2012 President CAPS Edmonton

PS: *I have often wished I had videos of my early speeches from Toastmasters. I tried so hard to be 'motivational', to encourage; and what I did was preach. I was stiff, didn't move, and came across as knowing it all.*

I remember someone saying "You should smile more." I thought I was, but **I was so focused on 'being' that I was not allowing myself to 'become'.** *Later, I started relaxing and allowing my fun side to show. That was when I started connecting with my audiences. I realized that it was not about me, it was about them. When I started focusing on them and allowed myself to be 'real' on stage it started coming together. They laughed with me and I started becoming more effective in sharing my ideas. Now, I do my homework and prepare my programs. Then I simply go on stage and play along with my audience.*

"You are as young as your faith, as old as your doubt; as young as your self-confidence, as old as your fear; as young as your hope, as old as your despair."
Samuel Ullman

Copyright and license notes

Speaking for $uccess
Applying mastery to your message and power to your presentation!

Bob 'Idea Man' Hooey, DTM, PDG, Accredited Speaker
2011 Spirit of CAPS recipient
Prolific author of 25 plus business and career success publications

Copyright 2012 Bob 'Idea Man' Hooey

ISBN 13: 978-1469932101   **ISBN 10: 1469932105**

Printed in the United States 10 9 8 7 6 5 4 3 2 1
1st edition printing - Fall 1998: **7th edition printing - Winter 2012**

Success Publications
Box 188 Mundare, AB T0B 3H0
www.successpublications.ca
Creative office: 780-736-0009

Acknowledgements and disclaimers

A very special dedication of this piece of myself, to the two people who meant the most to me, my folks **Ron and Marge Hooey**. Sadly, both my parents left this earthly realm in 1999. I still miss your encouragement and love. I was blessed with the two of you in my life.

To my inspiring wife and professional proof reader, **Irene**, who loves, encourages, and supports me in my quest to continue sharing my **Ideas At Work!** across the world. Thank you seems so inadequate for your work in helping make my writing and my client service better!

My thanks to the many people who have encouraged me in my growth as a leader, speaker, and engaging trainer in each area of expertise including **Speaking for Success**.

- To my colleagues and friends in the National Speakers Association **(NSA)**, the Canadian Association of Professional Speakers **(CAPS)**, and the Global Speakers Federation **(GSF)** who continually challenge me to strive for success and increased excellence.
- To those speakers and leaders within our industry whose ideas and skills I have observed and shared in this publication.
- To my many Toastmasters friends and family around the world, to whom I owe an un-payable debt of gratitude for your investment, encouragement, and support when I was just starting down this path; and oh, so rough around the edges.
- To my great audiences, students, coaching clients, and readers across the globe who share their experiences and enjoyment of my work. Your positive and supportive feedback encourages me to keep working on additional programs and publications like this one. My experience with you creates the foundation for additional real-life experiences I can take from the stage to the page or the classroom.
- My thanks to a select few friends for your ongoing support and constructive abuse. You know who you are. ☺

We have not attempted to cite all the authorities and sources consulted in the preparation of this book. To do so would require much more space than is available.

The list would include departments of various governments, libraries, industrial institutions, periodicals, and many individuals. Inspiration was drawn from many sources in the creation of Speaking for Success.

Disclaimer

This book is written and designed to provide information on more effective presentations and **Speaking for Success**. It is sold with the *explicit* understanding that the publisher and/or the author are **not** engaged in rendering legal, accounting, or other professional services. If legal or other expert assistance is required, the services of a competent professional in your geographic area should be sought.

It is not the purpose of this book to reprint all the information that is otherwise available to new, emerging, or established speakers; trainers or facilitators; sales professionals; and/or leaders. Its primary purpose is to complement, amplify, and supplement other books and reference materials.

You are encouraged to search out and study all the available material, learn as much as possible, and tailor the information to your individual needs. This will help to enhance your success in being a more effective leader, powerful speaker, or sales professional.

Every effort has been made to make this book as complete and as accurate as possible within the scope of its focus. However, there *may be mistakes,* both typographical and in content. Therefore, this book should be used only as a general guide or primer and not as the ultimate source of information. Furthermore, this book contains information that is current only up to the date of publication.

The purpose of **Speaking for Success** is to educate and entertain; perhaps to inform and to inspire. The author and publisher shall have **neither** liability **nor** responsibility to any person or entity with respect to any loss or damage caused, or alleged to have been caused, directly or indirectly, by the information contained in this 'primer' manual or book.

We trust you will find benefit in what we share and that, when applied, you will find your presentation skills will improve and your confidence as well.

Table of Contents

How to get the best use from Speaking for Success

Speaking for Success contains a range of tips, techniques, and ideas which can help you improve the way you create and deliver oral presentations. **It was not originally created as a book**, but as a course guide for programs delivered by the author in various BC colleges. It evolved to its present form with the inclusion of stories and first-hand experience based on copious conversations and observations of fellow professional speakers; as well as my own experiences in speaking across North America and the globe.

This is not just a book for casual reading. It is a book to be used, to be dipped into, and to be used as a resource or reference guide. It is your resource, so mark it, highlight it, and make notes in the margins. **To get the best from this book**, first visit the Table of Contents to identify which chapters and topics meet your needs. Read them carefully and make sure you understand the guidelines and advice given. Some of the topics may not be of direct interest to you, depending on your needs. You may wish to read some of the other chapters so that you can understand the needs of other speakers or scenarios where presentations are given.

Speaking for Success does not contain ALL the answers. It is a collection of thoughts, tips, techniques, lessons learned, and ideas shared from one speaker's viewpoint, mine. It is simply intended as an aid to your reflection, learning, and inspiration – a resource that you can draw upon in preparation for your presentations. Its aim is to give you a resource that, when applied and practiced in real presentations, will help you develop and build both your confidence and competence as a presenter.

I'd recommend that a productive approach for its use would be to take the tips and concepts presented here and blend them with your own style, personality, and creativity. Keep in mind your own time constraints and "comfort zone as a presenter," to generate unique and personalized ideas on how you can create, give, and improve your presentations.

This book is designed to offer you flexibility in terms of how you use it.

1) You can sit down for an hour or two and read it **cover to cover**. This is a great way to start by getting a feel for what is included, especially for newer or beginning speakers who want to gain the full benefit from their investment.

A word of advice:
Speaking for Success is the result of over 20 years of study and 15 plus years first-hand experience on the stage, in the classroom, and coaching executive clients. It might seem overwhelming or a bit confusing at first with the range of information we've included here. Once you have done a quick read the whole book, I suggest you then identify particular sections or tips that interest you and work on more manageable chunks at a time.

2) You can select one **chapter** or **section** at a time and work to incorporate the ideas you find into your own presentation style.

3) You can look at the **Table of Contents** and jump straight to the tips or areas of study that particularly interest you.

We have attempted to incorporate something of benefit for everyone, regardless of your current level or skill in public speaking. You might even find some contradictory advice in different parts of the book! This is because there is no single, universal **"right answer"** – you must find what is right for you, your objective, and your audience's needs. What works for you is what is best. Choose it, try it, and adapt it as needed to serve you in your quest to be a more powerful speaker.

"Effective speaking communicates the message in a way that makes it easier for the listener to relate and react positively to what they (listener) understand. Effective speaking is helped or enhanced by 'charting-a-course' to convey your message with impact."
Bob 'Idea Man' Hooey

Speaking for Success!
Applying mastery to your message and power to your presentation!

As you begin this journey, perhaps you might wonder, **"Why would I want to invest time to improve my speaking skills?"** The answers to these questions should provide some insight.

- Are you interested in learning thinking and communication skills that will **make a major difference in your long-term career** success?
- Are you interested in acquiring leadership and communication skills that will **develop your abilities** to more successfully work with other people and foster an enhanced sense of team?
- Are you interested in changing or **enhancing** your career?
- Would you like to learn an interviewing technique and enhance your confidence to **give you an edge on your competition**?
- Do you want to feel more **comfortable speaking** in any public situation?
- Do you have a **dream** of being a professional speaker, trainer, or facilitator?

Then, read on fellow traveler on the path of learning!

Why do some people succeed in advancing their careers while others do not? A decade or so back, AT&T commissioned California's Stanford University to conduct a survey to see if there were any reliable indicators.

Surprisingly, their results revealed that *"...the top predictors of success and upward mobility, professionally, were how much you enjoy public speaking and how effective you are at it!"*

Based on nearly 3 decades of leadership experience, this was no real surprise. Later, that same year, a report from Canadian Business Magazine mentioned 'their two indicators' were comfort in speaking and your ability to work with people. Frankly, the results would be similar if the study was done today.

People who become proficient at something that most of us fear tend to be noticed and often promoted!

According to the Book of Lists, **the number one fear** for most of us is speaking in public. (it has dropped in number recently) The old joke, *"Most people are so afraid of giving a speech they'd rather be in the casket than giving the eulogy!"* certainly still applies. Many people are uncomfortable expressing their thoughts in a public forum.

Additionally, those who confront their fear of speaking gain self-confidence. Their self-confidence filters through to other areas of their professional lives and actions. This happened time and time again with my students at various colleges. This material forms a part of my executive speech coaching sessions as well.

In fact, we've had the opportunity to share these ideas with leaders from some of Canada's 50 Best Managed Companies. I had the privilege of working with one CEO in writing and coaching his presentations when he received several business awards across Canada, North America, and the globe. I've seen it demonstrated even more dramatically in one-to-one coaching sessions or in small group settings. **Mastering this skill may very well be the '*pivotal*' point in your life and career.**

The focus here is to share some basic guidelines that will help you to improve your presentation skills as well as to help position you to succeed in your chosen field of endeavor. It will take **'work'** on your part; but it is worth the effort! No skill is ever acquired without concentrated and continuous effort on the part of the student. But, it can also be fun! What is shared here has been proven in the lives and improved abilities of thousands of professionals who've applied these guidelines and techniques.

In originally creating and now updating this **7th edition of Speaking for Success**, I drew again on my personal experience as a globe-trotting, *paid* professional speaker and trainer. I drew, as well, from my work and management background; and my extremely *(how did I ever survive without it!)* helpful experience and learning curve in Toastmasters International as well as NSA, GSF, and CAPS.

I un-ashamedly drew on the wisdom, notes, tips, examples, and techniques gleaned from my association with some of the world's top speaking professionals; members of NSA, CAPS, and GSF. Their examples taught and encouraged me to work harder.

I drew from **audience and platform PROVEN** techniques, as demonstrated in front of live audiences around the world that, with practice and application, you could turn into communication and career enhancement tools. I've seen them work when applied!

Most of you will not have the dream of being a professional speaker, as I did when I started down this path some 21 years ago. However, each of you can certainly learn to be more proficient from the examples of those who practice these results-oriented skills to earn their livelihood as professional speakers, facilitators, or trainers. I did and continue to do on a regular basis! School is never out for the true professional. We keep learning new lessons from our peers and our audiences.

Best-selling author, management guru, and successful speaker, Peter Drucker wisely forecast, ***"As soon as you move one step up from the bottom, your effectiveness depends on your ability to reach others through the spoken or written word."***

Learning and applying these platform techniques and audience-proven tips will prove invaluable as you pursue your new career or advance your existing position. They have certainly worked for me.

Effective communications training is a **"Foundation for Speaking Success!"** I continue to dedicate a significant portion of my time, study, and energy in learning, applying, and teaching these SIMPLE but POWERFUL techniques.

Speaking for Success has been a work-in-progress, designed as a stand-alone publication. Our 7th edition was rewritten and updated for this print edition. When I personally teach a presentation skills course or professionally coach a client, we use videos and lots of class participation as well as hands-on practice to augment it.

You can apply and practice these skills alone or by enlisting supportive friends or family to act as evaluators or a practice audience. Better yet, join a Toastmasters Club in your area. It's a great, cost-effective way to learn and reinforce these newfound skills with great people who are also learning.

For information on how to locate a club in an area near you, visit their website: **www.toastmasters.org** (Be sure to tell them Bob sent you!)

Perhaps you might attend a local NSA or CAPS Chapter meeting to observe and learn from some of the industry's top presenters. Visit **www.NSAspeaker.org** or **www.CanadianSpeakers.org** to find a chapter near you.

Your ability to speak in front of audiences will improve in **direct** proportion to the amount of time you invest to prepare and practice your skills. These skills are not learned *'just'* from a book, but from *'real life'* experience in front of an audience.

When I started down this path in April 1991 and joined my first Toastmasters Club, I realized the only way to improve would be in actually getting up and speaking. I made a commitment that if at all possible to never turn down an opportunity to speak. To date, other than scheduling conflicts, very few opportunities have been missed. It has helped immensely over the years!

Whether your desire is to simply overcome your fear of standing and delivering a presentation in front of an audience or stepping onto the stage as a *paid* professional speaker, these tips and techniques will form the foundation to see either desire fulfilled. Speaking can be fun *(yes, I said fun!)* if you've done your homework and keep your focus on the audience. The hard work is done before you walk on stage. Then you relax and play!

The *hardest* part of being a professional speaker is the work done before walking on stage to deliver your presentation. Once the homework is done, I simply get up and share my stories and messages with the audience. It gets easier as I apply my skills and refine my focus by making sure that what is shared is of value for the audiences. You can too!

Thanks again to the thousands of people in various paid audiences, Toastmasters Clubs, as well as my fellow CAPS, GSF, & NSA professional speakers for their investment in my life and growth as a speaker. I hope, in passing along the secrets we've shared, to partially repay their faith and contributions.

SPEAKING FOR SUCCESS!

I wish you a fun filled, life-long adventure, in following through on this major step you've undertaken in your personal and career success. It can be a richly rewarding journey, one that you will pause and reflect upon in years to come. You'll look back and see the significant changes you've made in your life, career, and your personal effectiveness. **Enjoy the journey!**

Bob 'Idea Man' Hooey, Distinguished Toastmaster
Accredited Speaker (48th in Toastmasters history)
2011 Spirit of CAPS recipient

Where do I stand now in my journey as a speaker?

Think about the last time you gave a presentation or spoke in front of a group (*however small*). Think back and give yourself some honest feedback on your performance and perceptions as a speaker or presenter. The key to a successful journey or goal is in accurately determining your starting point.

Someone asked me these types of questions at the start of my Toastmasters journey in 1991. I admit I said "No" to too many of them at that time. Each, however, points to a skill that can be easily acquired, polished, and applied.

Remember these questions are for your information only, so be honest.

DO I PRESENTLY...

		Yes	No
1.	Feel comfortable talking to other people?	___	___
2.	Have trouble explaining my views or ideas?	___	___
3.	Have nervous habits when I speak, such as saying um, uh Ok, you know, and ah, or fumbling with buttons, clothes, glasses, or change in my pocket?	___	___
4.	Focus on the audience's needs and interests when I make a presentation?	___	___
5.	Plan my presentations with a clear purpose in mind?	___	___
6.	Appear to be natural and sincere when I'm speaking?	___	___
7.	Listen carefully and analytically to other speakers?	___	___

8. Feel comfortable receiving feedback from others?   ___   ___

9. Offer feedback in a constructive, positive way that
    doesn't cause others pain or embarrassment?   ___   ___

The answers to these questions may prove to be the guideposts to the specific areas that you need to learn and the skills you need to apply in your pursuit to become a powerful presenter. It might be a good idea to come back several times as you proceed through this course of study and evaluate your progress.

Apply yourself and practice the techniques in this book and **you'll be amazed with the results!**

You'll see this success key periodically while reading this book. *I'll add additional tips, techniques, and stories, just for you. We'll also include a few more quotes to inspire you and give you something to think about.*

"WORK ...Nothing worthwhile comes easily. Half effort does not produce half results, it produces no results. Work, continuous work and hard work, it is the only way to accomplish results that last."
Hamilton Holt

Entertaining & special occasion presentations

You may never dream of becoming a professional speaker, but if you are reading this you most likely want to be more comfortable when you are called on to speak. You may encounter some of these opportunities to give specialized presentations. The basics covered in **Speaking for Success** will certainly apply for each of these examples.

You need to be aware of these different types of speeches and realize **their objectives determine and influence their format.** Knowing that helps you craft and deliver more effective presentations.

- **Introductions:** You might be called on to introduce a speaker, facilitator, or trainer brought in to do a presentation.
- **Welcome presentations:** You might also be called on to say a few words if a group visits your workplace.
- **Acceptance speeches:** Imagine you've just been honored or given an award.

*Recently (Nov. 28th, 2011) I was surprised with the highest honor given by the Canadian Association of Professional Speakers – **The Spirit of CAPS award**. As I headed up to the stage, I worked to calm myself and collect my thoughts. While we were taking pictures, my mind was grasping for the words to express how I felt at that moment. Visit: **www.ideaman.net/SoC.htm** to view the award presentation and my impromptu acceptance speech.*

- **Inauguration speech:** You've just been elected to a leadership role in a volunteer group and are called on to say a few words following the election.
- **Eulogies:** This can be an emotionally challenging role, if you were close to the person who has recently passed away and are called to say a few words about their life.

I remember choking back my own tears as I said good bye to my dad while watching my mom silently crying in the audience. I spoke from the heart about Dad as a man, as a father, as a compassionate caring person, and as a role model.

- **Toastmaster/MC:** Perhaps you are called on to MC or are the Toastmaster at a wedding or an award ceremony.

I had the privilege of doing this for two of our friends last year (2011) and was able to work in some special 'fun' pieces just for them.

- **New employee orientations:** Perhaps your employer will ask you to help orient new hires.

When I was part of the opening management team for the 1st two BC, Home Depots, we used to take turns doing this for new hires to outline what we expected and help them settle into our culture.

- **The farewell speech:** Stepping down from a leadership role leaving a long term position in a company or group – you might want to say a few words of thanks and reflect on the time you spent and the people who enriched your life.

Each of these unique presentation scenarios has a different focus and purpose and would then be structured and delivered appropriately. If presented with an opportunity of doing one of these:

- Take a minute to decide what you actually want to accomplish.
- Give some thought on how to structure it to best reach that goal or objective.
- **Treat each as an opportunity to practice and polish your skills**.
- Treat each as an opportunity to expand your toolbox of experience in front of an audience.
- You will grow, only by stretching and expanding past your comfort zones.

Speak to inspire! *"What is our aim? I answer in one word. Victory – victory at all cost, victory in spite of all terror, victory, however long and hard the road may be; for without victory, there is no survival."*
Winston Churchill

Qualities of an EFFECTIVE leader, speaker, trainer, or coach

Becoming an effective leader, facilitator, speaker, trainer, or coach means learning to draw on your abilities and skills to train those who need your help. Since I moved into the realm of professional speaking and training, I've learned first-hand the importance of these traits. **Communication is a critical skill in each of these roles.**

I have been diligently working to enhance them in my own efforts as a leader and trainer as well as a presenter. In addition to my speaking, training, or facilitation roles, they work very well in management situations, on the job, and in the co-ordination, motivation, and management of volunteers and direct reports as well.

Interestingly enough, many of these traits are demonstrated by the top leaders across North America; which is why 'leader' is in this list. As a speaker, trainer, coach, or facilitator part of what we are doing is leading and guiding our audiences. Here are some of the **traits of successful and *effective* leaders, speakers, trainers, and coaches.**

Good Communications Skills

- Use clear and concise language to instruct, direct, and coach
- Use active listening skills to draw them out and fully understand them
- Maintain eye contact

Solid understanding of the subject

- Comprehensive understanding of the subject or skills
- Willingness to draw from your background as a bridge or foundation to teach
- Willingness to grow and update your professional development

Experience

- It helps if you have done the job personally (*and well would be good, too*)
- Previous experience in speaking, facilitation, or training

Patience

- New people often make mistakes while they learn
- It often takes a few tries to get it right (*keep up encouragement*)
- Remember how it was for you when you started out?

Interest in being a trainer, speaker, facilitator, etc.

- You need to *seriously* enjoy helping people
- Seeing people grow and learn makes you feel good
- Seeing others' success gives you a sense of pride and satisfaction

Genuine respect for other people

- People view you as being knowledgeable *(and you model it)*
- People view you as being trustful and trustworthy *(you've earned it)*

Well-developed sense of humor

- You see the humor in the situation *(and you express it)*
- You don't take yourself or life too seriously *(you lighten it)*
- It helps you deal with some of the *'challenges'* of training and working with people. ☺

Having these traits and skills won't *guarantee* your success as a leader, facilitator, speaker, trainer, or coach. However, they will give you a better chance to do the job effectively enroute to greater success.

If you are committed to building your career and/or want to move into speaking or training, or are already a speaker or trainer, then these traits need to be a solid part of how you live your life in that role.

The more you demonstrate these traits, the more your audiences and teams will respond to your leadership, and the more productive they will become. If your role is already that of a leader, these skills will enhance it dramatically.

*"I hear
and I forget.*

*I see and I
remember.*

*I do and I
understand!"*

Confucius

These *wise words* were written thousands of years ago and yet they ring just as true in our 21st century lives and evolving business endeavors.

We *best equip* those we lead with use-it-now information, practical tools, and applicable actions; *when we facilitate* them in getting their hands *dirty* or in actually getting up and using what we provide.

For example: In our presentation skills training or executive speech coaching programs the quicker our students or clients up speaking, the better they learn and accelerate their learning curve.

Consider the thousands of Toastmasters around the world who *nervously* start speaking and find that their confidence and competence increases in *direct* relation to how often they are in front of an audience and in how they *apply* the feedback received.

Becoming an effective presenter is **not** learned *exclusively* from a book or by observing others in action. It is essentially a learn-as-you-do project. Kind of like life!

My challenge for you is to revisit what you are doing for your own learning curve, as well as those you work with. See where you can adapt it to add more *hands on* experience. How can you make it more experiential to anchor the learning and enhance the skill?

Three keys to 'successful' speeches

In public speaking, the cardinal rule to being truly effective is **"NEVER BE BORING!"** But, how do we do this when we are nervous and under *pressure to perform?*

I've been teaching my clients and various classes that the **"three keys to speaking success"** are based on acquiring the knowledge you need to successfully capture their attention, connect with your audience, and achieve your shared objectives.

Those three keys to speaking success are:

- **KNOW** your subject or topic
- **KNOW** your audience
- **KNOW** yourself

If you **know your subject** and are thoroughly prepared, you will be much more relaxed and effective than if you are 'winging' it.

Taking time to organize and delve into your topic will give you a sense of the depth you bring to the platform. It will also give you much more information than you will be able to deliver, which gives you back-up information for additional presentations and questions. This confidence, based on acquired knowledge, works wonders in helping to keep the "butterflies flying in formation," as we used to say in Toastmasters.

If you **know your audience**, you will be better prepared to effectively analyze their needs and select from the body of knowledge you've acquired on your topic to serve or solve those needs.

The better you know their backgrounds, history, connections, education, gender, and their ages; the better you will be able to construct and deliver your presentation in a way that is interesting, relevant, and informative to them.

If you **know yourself**, you can draw on your own experiences and build on your own strengths in developing your own speaking style.

You can share your own ideas and 'unique' stories in a way that allows you to be most effective. Self-knowledge is a tool of effective and successful communication.

Continually ask yourself, *"If I was in the audience, why would I be interested in this point or topic?"* Then simply make sure you have a good answer for that question. Your audiences are people, just like you. The better you know yourself, the better equipped you are to effectively reach them.

By skillfully combining your knowledge of self, your subject, and your audience, you will effectively increase your impact. You will also expand your impact as a presenter, interviewee, or speaker.

A final note here:

Be sure to apply the **3 P's of public speaking –
PREPARATION, PRACTICE, and PERFORMANCE!**

There is no substitute for being prepared, by practicing until you are certain that you are ready to present your material in a confident manner. Anyone who says they just get up and *fake it* is leading you down the wrong path. Prepare, practice, and polish and, then, confidently walk on stage and *play* with the audience. That is what I have learned to do and it works well for me.

The masters *only* make it look easy. They have put in the time, far from the public eye, long before they are introduced… and it shows!

Share your dreams, take some risks!
"Twenty years from now you will be more disappointed by the things you didn't do than by the ones you did do. Explore. Dream. Discover."
Mark Twain

Introducing a speaker

Introducing a speaker is a *specialized* form of presentation. Your role as the MC or introducer is tremendously important to the success of the speaker. I coach my introducers so they will understand the importance they play in my delivering the best performance.

- As the MC you have the awesome responsibility for helping the speaker **begin with a kick-start!**
- You set the tone, establish their credibility, build a bond between the audience and speaker, and answer these important questions for the audience.

Often they are thinking them, so why not answer these questions during the speaker's introduction?

- **Why this speaker?**
- **Why this topic?**
- **Why this audience?**
- **Why now?**

Exercise: To learn and to begin speaking and to understand the importance of a good introduction.

Recruit a partner and spend a few minutes interviewing along the following lines. Then change off and be the interviewee. When you are done, take turns introducing each other to an audience of your peers.

- **Name?**

- **Favorite color, food, or hobby?**

- **Why interested in becoming a better speaker?**

- Secret – i.e., something we don't know about them?

- Best thing learned so far in life?

- What they hope to learn from Speaking for Success?

You can change the questions to be more relevant to your situation. Perhaps getting some information about their hobbies, career, company, or community involvement would work.

"It's the little things that make the big things possible. Only close attention to the fine details of any operation makes the operation first class."
J. Willard Marriott

W. Clement Stone, who built a billion dollar *sales* organization out of the depths of the great depression (*early 1900's*), shared a *key* quote that has been close to my own growth and success. He worked with Napoleon Hill, who authored, **Think and Grow Rich**, published **Success Magazine**, and mentored Og Mandino, who authored motivational classic, **The Greatest Salesman in the World.**

Stone wrote: **"Little hinges swing big doors."** Successful, entrepreneurial leaders and great speakers constantly search and are open to finding the next "*slight edge*," the next profitable idea, or '*little hinge*'. I do too!

Travelling North America, I share a few basic ideas or messages with my audiences. One of them is, **"Once people fully understand the 'Why?' (purpose) the 'How's?' (processes or procedures) tend to take care of themselves."** Simple little idea, isn't it? However, these *little* things seem to slip the grasp of many of our North American leaders. We tend to complicate things. What little hinges have you applied in your life to open big doors or opportunities? What hinges have you used to leverage your speaking and leadership skills and expertise to better your career, company, or community?

Prepare yourself to WIN!

"I hated every minute of training, but I said, 'Don't quit. Suffer now and live the rest of your life as a champion.'" Muhammad Ali

 Building a successful leadership, sales career, or business takes hard work and applied energy. Becoming a competent, confident speaker does too. Success as a speaker follows a similar path. If it was that easy, everyone would be doing it. Sometimes you will reach the end of your strength or run head-on into a roadblock or wall – stay the course and continue.

You **can live the rest of your life as a champion.**

- A champion of your **creativity**.
- A champion of your **courage**.
- A champion of your **causes** and concerns.
- A champion of your sales team and your **clients**.
- A champion of living and sharing your **message**.
- A champion of your successful **career** path.
- A champion of your **dreams** (turning them into reality).

This is something experienced first-hand. I worked to overcome serious challenges and difficulties to prepare for the first level audition while working towards the Accredited Speaker designation. There were times I thought about throwing in the towel. When I spoke in San Diego (1995) and was not successful, I pulled myself up and worked harder for my opportunity to speak the following year in Saint Louis (1996).

When I again fell short, I was tempted to quit. I was frustrated, disappointed in my performance, and inclined to move on; to forget my dream of becoming a professional speaker. But, something would not let me quit! My success team would not let me quit either. They believed even when my belief wavered.

In 1998, when I walked across a Palm Desert, California stage to become the 48th person in the world to earn this coveted professional level Toastmasters' Award, I felt like a champion who had gone 10 rounds and emerged bloodied, but unbeaten. The applause and cheers of 2000 plus fellow Toastmasters still echo in my ears. It was a pinnacle point in my life as a speaker; the first of many.

Was it the three speeches I prepared and presented on the world stage that earned this award? Partially! Looking back, I believe it was the hundreds of prepared presentations given in various Toastmaster clubs and in community events across the country, as well as for paying clients that built the foundations for this eventual success on the world stage.

You can succeed in whatever field you enter if you are willing to prepare. You can become a top performing professional; be the champion you were meant to be. If I can do it, so can you!

The **Indiana University Hoosiers** basketball team were proven winners. They remained undefeated throughout their 1976 season and captured the NCAA National Championship under coach Bobby Knight. The '60 Minutes' commentator asked him about this amazing feat and why they were so successful. He asked, "*Was it their will to succeed?*"

"*The will to succeed is important,*" replied Knight, "*but I'll tell you what is more important –* **it's the will to prepare***. It's the will to go out there every day, training and building those muscles and sharpening those skills.*"

- Want to be a champion sales person? – **Prepare**
- Want to be an effective leader? – **Prepare**
- Want to create a profitable and winning business? – **Prepare**
- Want to be a powerful presenter or speaker? – **Prepare**
- Want to live an effective and meaningful life? – **Prepare**

Bill Bradley (scholar, basketball star, and former US Senator) reminds us, "*When you are not practicing, remember someone somewhere is practicing; and when you meet him or her, they will win.*"

Prepare, practice, and act decisively when the time is right! Prepare and make this your time to win!

Benchmark project
"So tell me about yourself?"

For many years I had the pleasure of teaching presentation skills in several lower mainland BC colleges. I had a wide range of students who were there to learn how to confront their fears, construct their thoughts, and speak without mumbling and fumbling. They wanted to be able to speak more powerfully and successfully. I would give them exercises so they would have the opportunity first hand of speaking in public. Over the years literally hundreds started speaking with nervousness and left with increased confidence and competence in their presentation skills. Bravo!

This is one of those exercises. They would have 5-10 minutes of class time to prepare and then we would have each member of the class present. Now some of you are saying to yourselves, ***"Bob, 10 Minutes... that is not enough!"*** Truth be told, that is just about right for this simple exercise. The objective is not to *over think* it or dig in too deep, but to organize your thoughts and speak on a subject you know well (YOU) for about 2 minutes.

Objectives of this exercise:

- Introduce yourself to a small group or class.
- Establish a beginning point or *benchmark* of your speaking skills and development to date. This will give you a reference point to chart your progress and growth as you continue to hone your **Speaking for Success** skills.
- Start speaking before an audience.
- Begin working on channeling or controlling your nervousness.

Suggested time: TWO minutes

Using this project to set a base line can be very helpful for you as well as to anyone who is sharing this material. This project gives you an opportunity to get up and try your skills and evaluate them for future growth and polishing.

The guiding rule is, **"…whatever you do is ok!"** as this is simply a starting point for your development into a more confident and articulate presenter. **The topic is one subject on which you are the expert – YOU!**

Obviously, in only two short minutes you can't paint too broad a picture, but you can share enough with your audience so they will get a sense of 'you' as a person. You might consider taking a historical base for your talk, i.e. birthplace, education, or family involvement.

You might share how you came to be interested in the profession you're pursuing or your job experience or share some of your ambitions or dreams. If you'd like to avoid using an autobiographical style, you might want to talk about your hobbies, sports, or anything that specifically relates to who you are as an individual.

You might even want to take this as a practice time for interview skills and create a verbal answer or crafted self-promotion to the question, **"So, tell me about yourself?"**

Take 5-10 minutes to prepare your talk. Keep it simple and don't try to memorize it. The concept behind starting with **"YOU"** is to allow you to talk about a topic on which you are truly the expert. Choose something you know very well!

A few tips: Select your points wisely for their impact. Keep in mind the concept of using an opening, body development, and conclusion. Try to capture your audience's attention with your opening statement. Remember that this talk is in front of friends, family, or people who are learning alongside you; people who will be supportive of your efforts. Share something of common interest to help minimize your nervousness.

Remember to breathe! Relax and enjoy this; have fun!

If you are using notes, try not to hold them. Place them down so you can refer to them *when* necessary. Since you are talking about yourself, relax and try not using notes. You might just surprise yourself and your audience.

PS: This is a great exercise to get ready for an interview. Often your interviewer will ask you to tell them about yourself. This is a great opportunity to smoothly transition into a 2 minute commercial on why they should hire or select you for the position. **Enjoy the journey!**

How to handle your nervousness

Here are a few easily applied ideas on how to handle and overcome your nervousness:

1. **Don't fight it!** Realize that being a *little* nervous is normal. I accept that and allow that nervous energy to propel me to a more impactful presentation.
2. Being **mentally prepared** is a good part of winning and Speaking for Success. Being physically prepared is another aspect of the journey.
3. Do something **physical** to work out the nervous energy.
   - Take a brisk walk.
   - Don't sit with your legs or arms crossed.
   - Let your arms dangle at your sides while you're sitting waiting to speak.
   - While your arms are dangling, twirl your wrists so your fingers shake loosely.
   - Pretend you're wearing a heavy overcoat or jacket and feel it on your shoulders as your shrug them up and down.
   - Waggle your jaw back and forth a few times to loosen it up. This relaxes your face and allows you to speak better and be heard.
   - Deep breathing can help, but don't hyperventilate.
   - Use the power of self-talk, say, 'Let's go!' or use some of the affirmations I share with you later in this Speaking for Success manual.

Don't be self-conscious about having a warm up routine. Champion athletes do warm ups because they know it helps them prepare to do their best. It also reduces the chance of injury. Warming up allows you to be at your best in front of an audience. It also allows you to loosen up and be more relaxed. Find out what works for you and build it into your preparation routine.

Here is a mental tip: Nervousness and '*being excited*' are two sides of the same equation. Mentally move into the '*being excited*' about the opportunity you have to share your ideas and to positively influence this audience's lives for the better!

Bob's Foundations for Speaking Success

When this material is taught in person, one of the areas covered as an overview is what I call my **"Foundations for Speaking Success!"**

Investing time to make sure you have completely thought through and answered these questions is essential to your confidence and success on the platform. These ideas were gleaned from conversations with fellow professional speakers. I've added to their wisdom from my own first-hand experience. These "*foundations*" have worked for me and **they will work for you!** The knowledge gleaned from their *wisdom* is the secret to being able to walk confidently up to the front and deliver a message that means something to my audiences.

The secret in making sure the audience gets the best presentation possible, with the most value, blended with personal stories and teaching points, **is in the pre-preparation**. This is what you do well before you start crafting your presentation.

Questions, thoughtful questions like these, can be the keys that unlock the door to success in any venture. This is no less true if your desire is to be a confident speaker, who connects with his or her audience, and leaves them wanting more.

- **WHY** are you speaking?
- **WHAT** do you want to accomplish?
- **WHO** is your audience?
- **WHEN** will you be speaking?
- **HOW** long will you be speaking?
- **WHERE** will you be speaking?
- **WHAT** tools will you use?

WHY ARE YOU SPEAKING?

- **Major theme.** What is it and why is it of importance to the audience? What is the central theme you wish to speak about? Why would it be of interest to an audience, especially this one? Is there a theme or major message your client would like you to deliver?

- **What moves YOU?** What motivates you to want to speak about this topic?
- **Experience.** Do you have some relevant experience that qualifies you to speak on this topic? What do you bring to the platform? How does your experience prepare you to share this message? How does it prepare you to understand their needs and build a bond with them?
- **Credibility.** Why "YOU" and not someone else? Do you have some academic, unique, or special job related qualifications that lend support to you as a speaker? Have you done your homework in making sure you've fully researched and prepared for this presentation and this audience?
- **Background.** How does your background prepare you to speak to this group? Are there shared or common elements in your background that give you a sense of what would be most helpful to those in your audience?

Answering these questions is a key to reinforcing your confidence and presentation skills. It will allow you to speak with greater conviction and passion. Make sure '*you*' are the person who is well qualified and prepared for the presentation. Believe me, it helps!

WHAT DO YOU WANT TO ACCOMPLISH?

In 1991, when I first joined Toastmasters, our manuals outlined various speaking projects that allowed us to focus on a particular goal in our speaking. Being able to know what end result to shoot for helped me in preparing more effectively. Here are some of the speaking goals recalled from the various manuals:

- **Speaking to inform?** Do you have a new policy, procedure, or point of information to pass on to the audience? How do you make sure they understand and apply it?
- **Speaking to persuade?** Do you have a passion for something and want them to change direction or follow you in making a change? Do you want them to buy from you, hire you, or promote you? How do you convince them you are the best person for the job?
- **Speaking to entertain?** Is it your primary purpose to help them have an enjoyable time; to make them laugh and forget their troubles for a bit? This is a very tough way to speak, but if you do it well, you can enhance your career.
- **Speaking to inspire or motivate?** Is your purpose to inspire them, to lift their spirits, to encourage them to try again or a little harder?

What specifically would you like them to feel empowered to do when you are finished speaking?

- **Speaking with a call to action?** Do you have a specific goal in mind that you'd like them to help you with? Do you want them to sign up, step up, or join you in taking a stand or an action?
- **Some other objective?** What specifically is it you want them to get from your presentation?

Be clear about the results or goal in mind, while making your presentation is essential. Being able to pull the relevant information together will make your points come alive!

Be clear in what result you desire, what you want the audience to get from your presentation, or what action you want the audience to take.

As someone once said, *"If you don't know where you're going, any road will get you there!"*

WHO IS YOUR AUDIENCE?

- **Age ranges.** Knowing their age ranges will be helpful in preparing and selecting stories, illustrations, and other supportive material. It will also help you determine how to structure your presentation for maximum effectiveness.
- **Gender Mix.** Are you speaking to a group of men? A group of women? A mixed group? How many of each? Knowing this will help you present your message so it appeals effectively to both genders and ensures it will be understood in relation to their mind-set. It will also help you select examples or stories that are relevant.
- **Backgrounds.** What do you know about these people? What do they do for a living? What educational background do they have? What ethnic or family backgrounds do they have? Do you have any common backgrounds, connections, or experiences with them that you can draw or build on?
- **Common bonds.** Do they share any common experiences, bonds, or backgrounds? Are they all parents? Members of a special group? Volunteers? Do you have any connection with this common bond you can draw or build on?
- **Reason they are attending?** Knowing why they are in the audience can be very important in your preparation. It is a foundation to making sure you present your message to maximize your chances of having them take it in.

33

Are they there because the topic is of interest to them or someone close to them? Are they there because they've been told to show up, by a boss or other authority figure? Is attendance a reward or punishment? **Makes a big difference!**

Knowing your audience is one of the essential keys in presenting a great speech. Knowing them allows you to present the information most helpful to them. Doing your research in getting to know your audience can make a major difference. *Before undertaking any speaking engagement, I make it a point to talk in advance to some of the people who will be in the audience.*

WHEN WILL YOU SPEAK?

- **Time of day.** Make sure you know when in the day you'll be speaking. If you are speaking later in the afternoon or following a heavy meal, you will have a more difficult time with the audience. Early mornings can be difficult, too!
- **On the program.** Are you speaking as a keynote or opening general session? Are you following 2-hour happy hours and a big meal? Plan accordingly.
- **In relation to other speakers.** Are you sandwiched between other speakers? Do you follow another speaker? Who are they? What will they be speaking on? Find out about your fellow speakers and their topics. Be prepared to adapt or change your presentation, stories, or jokes.

At one engagement, I was to follow Alberta's Lt. Governor Lois Hole. The organizer asked that I be ready to adjust my time as Her Honor was known to go over once in a while. I stood at the back of the room as she was piped in and watched in amazement as she stopped to hug people on her way in.

She was pretty close to her time. I was happy to adjust my remarks following this wonderful lady, who was a credit to the Province of Alberta. I was asked to speak on her behalf years later when she was suffering from chemo and the death of her husband. Also, an honor.

- **Date and time.** Make sure you know exactly when and what day you are speaking. Make sure you confirm it closer to the date. Seems a simple thing, but I know more than one professional speaker who missed an engagement when they neglected to confirm and showed up *'late'* due to a change. Don't schedule too close to the event start either.

Early in my speaking career, I remember landing in Omaha barely 45 minutes before I was scheduled to speak, to find a very concerned client. Bad weather and a mechanical breakdown on two of my flights wiped out a 4-hour window and brought me close to missing my presentation. Now I travel well in advance to make sure I am there; rested and ready to give my best.

The time and position on the agenda can affect your audiences' ability to respond or retain your message. You need to be aware of those factors and make changes to give yourself the best chance of effectively delivering your message and having it heard.

HOW LONG WILL YOU SPEAK?

Consider your audience. Have you ever been sitting on a hard chair, butt aching, eyes hurting, back straining while listening to a speaker drone on and on, oblivious to the time and the audience? Put yourself in their position and make sure you structure your time wisely for maximum interest and benefit for them.

Organize your presentation. Knowing how long you speak will allow you to organize your thoughts to make sure they flow logically. Also, if you have a shorter time period, you will need to get to the point quicker and support it with fewer relevant points. If you are speaking longer, you'll need to **consider the following points in constructing your presentation.**

- **5-7 minute segments:** consider the attention span of your audiences and try to design your presentation in smaller segments. People traditionally need a change of pace every 5-7 minutes, so schedule or structure your presentation accordingly. Wonder if this was why most of our Toastmasters projects were 5 to 7 minutes?
- **Group participation exercises.** If you are planning a longer presentation, please incorporate some group work. This will allow you to take mini-breaks and allow your audiences to have a change of pace. You'll all appreciate it!
- **Consider audience involvement.** Regardless of the length of your presentation, having audience participation is a key to making your message work. Ask questions? Get them to volunteer to help you demonstrate something, hand out something. Get them to briefly share with each other. Get them involved and keep them involved. More on this later.

Structure and time your presentation to maximize your impact takes planning and practice. The results are more than worth your effort!

WHERE WILL YOU SPEAK?

- **Location and logistics.** Make sure you know precisely where you will be speaking: location, address, how to get there, and any other logistics that make it work for you to be there ready and prepared to do your best.

One speaker friend actually found himself checking into his hotel in the wrong town the night before he was to speak. Same name, different state. This made for a long night of travel to be there for the next day. I'll bet from now on, he double checks the location.

Update: I remember laughing about his challenge. Years later, I had a client call me about an after dinner presentation in Portland. I looked at my schedule and saw I was speaking in Boise, Idaho for two days in the mornings. My thought, get a flight, fly over, deliver my speech, and fly back later in the evening or early the next morning. Or so, I thought! I told the client this and she laughed. She said, **"Bob, I am calling about speaking in Portland, Maine."** *I had thought she meant Portland, Oregon. Oops! With the time change, I would be late before I even left for the airport. I wasn't able to help her for that date, but she did hire me for the following year.*

- **Room layout.** How is the room laid out for your presentation? Give the organizer specific instructions if you need to set it up a special way for your presentation. Always get there at least 2 hours early in case it isn't set up. Sometimes you will have to make do. You can always make some changes to make it work a bit better for you and your audience. This is your responsibility – use it wisely.
- **Sound system needs and capability.** If you need one, is there one available? I'd suggest if you are speaking to any group larger than 40-50 people, it might be wise to have one. Make sure you arrive early enough to test it and know how to adjust it for comfort levels.
- **Audio-visual needs and location.** What audio-visual tools are available for use? Do you need them? Discuss this in advance with your meeting planner or the organizer and plan accordingly. Always have a backup plan when 'Murphy's Law' strikes and the tool you were planning on using isn't available.
- **Climate control.** Make sure you know where the climate controls are and how to adjust them or get help quickly. It is your responsibility to make sure your audience is comfortable.

You need to be aware of the logistics around where you are speaking. This allows you to prepare with confidence, by minimizing the *'little things'* that can worry you or detract you.

WHAT TOOLS WILL YOU USE?

- **Flip chart.** Is it visible to the audience? Use big letters, not too much on each page, and please use **colors** that your audience can see from anywhere in the room. Keep in mind, you may have color blind audience members. Flips charts are great for smaller groups and interactive sessions.

- **Computer and LCD projector.** Using PowerPoint or presentation slide software can make or enhance your presentation. Make sure it is simple, not crowded, and not too slick. Hint: don't be too dependent on the tools. They are there to reinforce your message and they sometimes go down or don't work.

- **TV and VCR.** Do you have video clips? Please cue them in advance and make sure the equipment is set up and ready to go when you need it. Again, make sure you've assigned someone to help. Today most of this is shared with your computer and an LCD projector, but the guidelines still work.

When I co-hosted the Cancun Wealth Creation Summit, we were lucky to have a professional Canadian crew for our filming. I worked out the film clips and camera cues in advance with one of the crew members. Amazing how much professionalism it added to our overall sessions. Make sure your audience can see the TV or big screen easily. **If it can't be seen, it shouldn't be used.**

- **Charts and posters.** Keep them simple and make sure they are readable from anywhere in the room. Make sure they are sturdy and positioned for easy access.

- **Slide projector. This can still be a good tool, although your computer often takes its place today.** Is it positioned correctly so everyone can see it? Make sure you've run through your entire presentation to make sure your slides are in the correct order and right side up.

- **Handouts/learning guides.** Make sure they are relevant to your topic. Give the audience a reason to take them home and use them or refer back to them. Decide in advance **when** you will hand them out. If they are not needed during the presentation for reference, handing them out at the end of your presentation would be better. Let your audience know they are coming.

- **Props.** Can be very effective tools in demonstrating a point or principle. Props work for keeping your audience involved in your presentation. Make sure they are positioned for easy access and are ready to go when you need them. Can everyone see them?

- **Costumes.** Would dressing to illustrate your topic be a benefit? It might, but consider it carefully. Make sure it enhances your message and credibility and doesn't become a distraction.

Selecting the proper tool to assist in making your presentation more powerful, more memorable, and more easily understood is an important element in your success. Always consider the size and layout of the room and the visibility of any tool you select.

If they can't see it, it won't work; and quite likely will detract from your overall presentation.

Never use a tool unless you've practiced with it in advance. Make sure you are proficient in its use. If you fumble on stage, you will lose your credibility and possibly the audience's attention.

Always have a plan 'B': Murphy's Law was designed for speakers. Make sure you have back-ups and know when and how to use them. If something goes wrong, simply move ahead and switch to plan 'B' as smoothly as you can. **Be professional!**

Don't be dependent on your tools!

Your audience is not there to *just* enjoy a multi-media presentation. They are there to hear you speak about something they hope will prove valuable in their lives and/or careers. Choose wisely, but don't be dependent on them. They are there to make you look good, reinforce or support your points, visually demonstrate a point, or simply help keep your audience involved in your message.

Don't forget **'you are the message'** and these tools are yours to use to enhance your ability to get that message out effectively.

The more *effective* speakers know how to leverage their tools wisely and professionally, so that the tools are not the focal point in their presentation. After all, you want them to walk out of the room talking about you or your topic, not the visuals.

Definition of the roles for trainers, facilitators, and keynoters

If we are to be *effective* in our roles as presenters, it is important to understand the similarities and differences that encompass the three major functions played by our CAPS members. (*Speakers in general.*) I realize many of you might not have the focus of becoming a professional; however, each of us can increase our professionalism when we present.

The Canadian Association of Professional Speakers defined the three major aspects of what our **'Experts Who Speak!'** actually do for their respective clients. Helps us make sense of the roles and the expected results.

My speaking journey began in classroom **training.** I still do quite a bit of that for professional associations and corporate clients across North America. I've had the privilege of training and coaching senior executives, CEO's, and Presidents from Canada's 50 Best Managed Companies.

Facilitation is another skill that draws on your speaking, listening, and thinking skills. You, as the facilitator, are the catalyst that allows the group to openly discuss and reach decisions.

More recently (last 6 or 7 years) I've been working more as a **motivational keynote speaker.** Interestingly enough this was the original goal and dream when I joined Toastmasters to hone and add to my skills, back in April of 1991.

Here are the three areas with explanations as to how they play out.

TRAINING

Desired result:	acquire, build or enhance 'success' skills
Communication style:	2-way between speaker and audience – interaction carries audience
Energy flow pattern:	between trainer & audience and among audience participants

Learning style:	primarily through activity, discovery, and interaction
Attention focus:	shared focus between audience and the trainer
Critical success factor:	new skill set or behaviour learned, plus commitment to apply or use it back home or on the job – **Ideas At Work!**
Presenter brings:	expertise in subject matter, skills (adult learning design of training), patience, explanation, demonstration, and feedback abilities

FACILITATION

Desired result:	bring group to a point of self-management of its own processes to achieve the results it chooses or desires
Communication style:	normally among group members themselves
Energy flow pattern:	generated by, and maintained by the group – boosted from time-to-time, by the facilitator
Learning style:	occurs through interaction, experimentation, and self-assessment
Attention focus:	group themselves – the facilitator is there to assist them!
Critical success factor:	group owns/takes responsibility for its' solutions and decisions, fresh awareness of its' nature, processes, and greater openness and trust
Presenter brings:	sensitivity to people and climate; here and now awareness; focus; willingness to intervene, challenge, and teach; flexibility; and patience

KEYNOTING

| Desired result: | motivate or inspire to action, provide context/meaning, set theme |
| Communication style: | 1-way, speaker generally carries the audience |

Energy flow pattern:	speaker to audience (more energy in short time – pushed)
Learning style:	occurs silently, individually, in the audience's head and heart
Attention focus:	the speaker, their message, and their delivery
Critical success factor:	a few key points – reinforced and driven home!
Presenter brings:	high energy and commitment; mastery of the platform; ability to evoke feelings, challenge thoughts and assumptions; and willingness to challenge audience to think, and to act!

As you can see, each of these presentation areas has its own focus, skill set, and critical success factors. Being aware of the differences and expectations for each area will assist you in your preparation and success!

 **Presentation tip:** Why would you want to take the extra time and effort it takes to make an effective presentation? What would it accomplish? What is your motivation for investing your time in researching, creating, or crafting and then practicing and honing it before you deliver it?

An effective presentation:

- Demonstrates that you are thoroughly prepared and have done your homework.

- Has its information well organized in a complete and concise format.

- Reveals your human side and acts as a catalyst to connect with your audience.

- Reveals your competency – demonstrates that you do indeed have the skill set and the ability to successful complete your assignment or project.

- Consistently keeps your audience awake and aware of your actions.

Getting to know your audience

At a 1999 NSA Platform Skills Lab training session, fellow speaker Steve Moroski from Atlanta, GA shared insights he'd picked up on *getting to know* his audiences. He shared some enlightening *'Trends'* that will affect how we prepare and how we present.

Steve encouraged us to open up a two-way flow between our audience and ourselves prior to walking on stage.

He suggested **a few ideas to increase this flow.**

- Kick-off call to organizer to make sure we know *'who'* is coming.
- Pre-program questionnaire to organizer and audience survey.
- Gap analysis to determine areas where training or additional skills might help.
- Conference call or calls with several people who are attending.
- Email from their leader telling attendees about upcoming session and inviting them to visit his website.
- Conversations on-site (*prior to your session*).
- Connecting and interaction during the session.

One of the keys to being effective on the platform is in knowing your audience. These are a few ways that I can attest work well in that regard.

There are a few Trends you should be aware of as well.

TREND 1:

Audiences today are very sociable. Schedule more frequent breaks and small group work. Throw out more questions. Allow them to share and dialogue among themselves. Encourage them to Tweet during your presentation. Give them something to Tweet about! ☺

TREND 2:

Audiences today don't read the papers. They expect to be entertained. Use props, audience involvement, stories, visuals, and more effective use of lights.

TREND 3:

Audiences today are risk takers. Take some risks yourself. Bring them up on stage. Challenge them in stories, programs, etc. They may not remember what you did, but they will remember how you made them feel and what you challenged them to think. Take risks to connect and challenge them to grow!

TREND 4:

Audiences today are more cynical. Use metaphors vs. gimmicks, allow for more laughter (*opens up the soul and allows you to share points*). Make your introductions more *relative* and applicable to them.

TREND 5:

Audiences today are tired of being talked at. Involve them! Use story holes (*e.g. People were (_____) 'amazed'*) and let them fill in the blanks. Look for opportunities to interact and to allow them to do so.

TREND 6:

Audiences today are suspicious, *of us and our promises*. Watch your clothing as well. Dress appropriately for credibility. Verbally come off the platform and the *pedestal*.

Honesty is important.
Tell the story behind the story. Tell the story you're not telling. Tell the struggles, the challenges that led to your eventual outcome. Being real is being honest and sharing accordingly.

TREND 7:

Audiences today are also more highly educated. They will check out websites and do their own on-line research. Show them how to use what you teach. Use everyday stories. Show them where it fits in their lives and careers and they will respond. Some of them will have researched your topic and might be more informed than you, unless you've done your homework.

What audiences know...
(without being told)

...how you feel that day

...if you don't like or respect them

...when you've memorized your presentation

...when you're lying or bluffing

...when you're giving them a sales pitch

...when you've given up on yourself

**Never underestimate the sensitivity
of your audience! Be open and let them in!**

Principles made personal yield powerful results - Ideas At Work!

Mastery of the message
Using the 3 M's of Speaking Success

I still remember the first experience of being in the 'magic of the moment.' We'd truly connected – my audience and I. They were with me fully, completely. I could take them where I wanted. WOW, what an experience! It was amazing, and nearly 20 years later, I can still vividly recall being in the moment (zone) with them and how it felt. Awesome!

Yes, I have been there since, and work to go there often, but the freshness of that experience lives on in my memory. It inspires and drives me to work diligently to prepare each session, to give my best, and to be fully there for my audiences.

That is the true 'mastery of the message' – as shown in the results and reactions of those who receive and act on it!

Mastery is an attainable skill; if you care enough and are willing to pay the price and put in the effort. I have carefully observed my CAPS, NSA, and GSF colleagues and speaker friends. I have watched those who are acknowledged *masters* on the platform and in the training room, to see what they do and what they bring to their mastery. Each has their own unique style and substance. Each has a shared commitment to mastery and serving their audience's highest needs.

So let's explore the **3 M's of Speaking Success™** that lead to the mastery of the message and give you entrance into the magic of the shared moment.

Message:

First of all make sure you have something to say!

This should be a given, but it isn't to many emerging speakers. All too often, I have seen beginning speakers who simply *parrot* something they've read or heard from another speaker or author. It is not real or relevant for them or for their audiences and sadly, it shows.

Not that sharing a message *gleaned* from a master or a group of masters is a bad thing. Presenting it as though it is your own is! It is unprofessional and borders on plagiarism or intellectual property theft. DON'T DO IT! Make sure you've *fully* researched your material so you have some depth and are not a 'book-report' speaker.

To reach your audience you need to *filter your message* through your life and your experiences to make sure it is real and relevant to them. If it is not real or relevant to you, it won't connect and you'll fail.

- How well do you know your audience? What do you know about them that would guide you in the research and the crafting of your message?
- How much time have they given you to share it?
- What gems of wisdom, what stories, what experiences can you draw on to flesh it out and make your message live, connect, and remain embedded in their hearts?
- What do you want them to learn, understand, or act on from your message?

Dig deep in your message and prepare well.

The masters never shirk their diligence in preparation!

Messenger:

You as the messenger bear a strong responsibility for the success of your message being received and acted upon by your audiences.

It needs to be fully integrated and involved in your life to become real and relevant to them. It needs to be in line with what you truly believe to be credible and even more importantly, achievable by action on their part.

They will believe your message and act on it, when they believe you!

What is your motive and motivation for speaking to them? It is important to know why you are speaking and where you are coming from, if you would seek to succeed with them, connect with them, and impact their lives.

Be honest with yourself in what you seek here. Do you seek to simply entertain yourself at their expense, use them for therapy? Or, are you seeking to impart and inspire them to gain knowledge, take action, and rally around the flag to a better life or a more effective career or business?

The masters know themselves and share openly and boldly!

Knowing yourself helps you take what you know about them and apply it in crafting your message and in more skillfully delivering it.

Method:

Actually, this is the *easier* part of the presentation equation. ☺

If you've dug deep enough to make sure what you have to say is truly valuable and has relevance to your audience, made sure it is in-line with your own integrity and life; it will be so much easier to communicate effectively to an audience.

Once you've decided what outcome you desire from the communication of your message, it is easier to structure the delivery system. Depending on the message and the desired outcome, *(and of course the time constraints of the time you have to deliver it)*, you can blend in stories, audience interaction and exercises, and inspirational bits.

Time is one of the biggest factors that impact the delivery method you chose.

I've grown to love the interaction with audiences. I find when keynoting, that my ability to incorporate active dialogue with them is more challenging than during breakouts and training sessions. That being said, I still work in some areas where they can actively feedback or respond to the message being shared.

Asking questions, getting them to share something with a neighbor, or simply using rhetorical questions to draw them in; all of these techniques will work in building a bridge to the hearts and minds of your audiences.

The effective use of storytelling is *under-rated* and ignored by speakers in many levels and arenas. Sometimes the most effective way to communicate a message is to wrap it tenderly in a story.

How many Sunday school lessons do you still remember; how many nursery rhymes or children's stories can you still recall? My bet, lots of them – and if you can recall the story, you can retain the lesson and the message behind the story.

The masters weave stories to last a lifetime!

A few final thoughts…

If you want to achieve the 'mastery of the message' you will need to dig deep to master yourself first and then draw from that in preparing and delivering your message. Applying the 3 M's will help you succeed.

You owe it to your audiences to diligently prepare and to bring forth your best. Anything else would be a waste of everyone's time and energy.

Seeking to become a master of the message is the beginning of attaining the mastery – and the journey is worth it!

Use story starters to warm up your brain. To get you started, I've included some of my own story starters. These story starters give my brain a mental kick and get me thinking about something I might put into an easy format to capture and share an idea. Perhaps they will work for you too?

How to:

- How I learned the importance of _____:
- How I got started in the _____ business.
- My worse Customer Service experience: why?
- My favorite customer: why?
- The best lesson I learned last year:
- Something funny happened to me:
- How to overcome _____:
- How to initiate _____:
- How to unravel the secret of _____:
- My dream company: why?
- The best lesson I've learned here at _____:

An open and closed case

The first time I created the hand illustration was in front of a class of students, some of them who had English as their second language. I told them, creating a speech, without notes, is as simple as… as your hand.

- The opening *(thumb)* is **telling your audience what you're going to tell them** or the central theme or objective of your presentation.
- The three points *(middle fingers)* illustrate, expand, develop, or support that theme. Simply, **telling them**. Cover the first point and then move on to each successive one. Depending on the time allotted, your points can be expanded or contracted, by adding additional stories, examples, or illustrations.
- The conclusion *(little finger)* reminds them of the central theme, summarizes the 3 points and of course **tells them what you've just told them.**

When you are speaking, *extra* attention needs to be given to crafting your openings and conclusions. Often people will only remember your opening statement or something you've said in closing. Accepting this trend in audience behavior as accurate, it makes sense to work a little harder on your opening and conclusions, to ensure they are tight and create pictures in your audience's minds. In fact, if you were to memorize these would be the two areas where it might be appropriate.

At a special NSA Platform Skills Lab in Tempe, AZ, one of our coaches, John Alston *(known for his ability to grab an audience with his openings)* shared a few thoughts on effective openings with us. I took copious notes.

John shared his three rules on creative, impactful openings:

1. **Get their attention and keep it!** *(By any means possible)* This sometimes means getting *outside* of your comfort zone to capture and keep their attention. If your message is worth sharing, it's worth being dramatic to give them a chance to hear it and you. John walked on the stage carrying a briefcase and proceeded to drop it with a loud bang which caught our attention for sure.
2. **Remain current and relevant with your content and context** – know your audience. *(Use surveys and reviews)*

If you are to effectively reach your audiences you need to go where they are – and that requires getting to know them. John shared the differences for example of speaking to young people vs. CEO's and how you would structure your opening to target either group.

3. **Find and exploit your common ground** – look for the universals. *(What do we have in common?)* Ask yourself what you have in common with your potential audience. Is there a universal principle that underlies that commonality? If so, can you build on that principle or idea? Often, this commonality is the secret to building a good rapport with your audience or a bridge to allow them to join you on your journey in words.

Good openings make or break your presentation and help establish a connection with your audience. We learned about openings when I joined Toastmasters twenty plus years ago. **Good openings incorporate some of these elements:**

- Tend to be short, punchy, and dramatic or thought provoking.
- Can contain a startling statement, position, intrigue, or a challenging question.
- Can incorporate an appropriate and relevant quotation, story excerpts, paradoxes, good and bad experiences, or a personal story or illustration.
- References a shared or common experience with your audience.
- Drawn from life, based on journalized stories, reading, listening to stories, and conversations with others.
- A general or *universal* statement that ties in or relates to your subject, while acting as an attention getter to draw them into your presentation.
- Visuals, a display, or an appropriate or relevant prop or picture.

As an audience member, you have about 30 seconds to capture my attention and draw me into the subject of your presentation. **Choose your opening words carefully.**

- Avoid weak or timid openings with trite questions like; "Do you ever wonder?" "How many of you have…?" *(These have been vastly overdone in my opinion)*
- Avoid a slow moving, lengthy statement or story that doesn't relate to your subject. Start fast and get us involved with your presentation.
- Avoid an apologetic statement or excuse such as *"I wasn't ready, but…"* **Never build a case against yourself or tell me you're not prepared… let me find out for myself!** ☺ Telling me you aren't prepared says, *"I'm not important enough for you to do your homework and prepare in advance to meet my needs."* It insults the audience.

- Don't open with a joke or humorous story unless you have it down cold. It needs to be relevant to the audience and supports your presentation.
- Don't waste the audience's time with stereotypical thank you's and general opening remarks. Get into the meat of your presentation and grab my mind and my heart!

Having said that; it is important to acknowledge the person who introduced you and the audience. Most of the time I see this overdone and it weakens your opening impact. Do it briefly and move on or start your presentation and then acknowledge them. Make sure they know you are planning it this way. Save it for a bit later, after you have me hooked into your presentation! Very much like a movie where they show a part of it and then show the titles before moving ahead to the rest of the film.

Keeping our attention is a challenge in itself. People can listen at 4-500 words per minute while we normally talk at 125-175 per minute. This leaves **a gap** that needs to be handled in the development of your presentation.

Remember to create vivid word pictures for our minds. If you don't, we tend to think or fantasize about other areas. We think about grocery lists, work undone, or even, I'm told; fantasize about *sexual* things when we are not involved mentally. I tell my students if they smile as they leave, at least I know they've had a good time. ☺ I work to verbally paint pictures that challenge them to think about what I'm saying and keep them actively involved in my presentation.

Similarly, **captivating closings** are critical to your success. **Effective closings also incorporate certain key elements:**

- Summarize your major speech points and the conclusion or action drawn from them.
- Bring them back to the main theme or purpose of your presentation.
- A relevant story, illustration, or quotation that re-emphasizes the major point or central theme of your presentation.

In addition to the above, my friend and co-author NSA Past President Mark Sanborn, CSP, CPAE shared some thoughts on what he called *Grand Slam* closings with us in Tempe. Again, I share what I recall and have applied in my own presentations.

Mark talked about ensuring that our closings were changed in focus from *Event to Experience*.

51

He challenged us to not simply close, but to help our audience's *experience* the completion of our speeches. He also challenged us to make sure our closings were an *integral* part of our presentation and not just slapped on as we ran out of time. They needed to be part of the flow of our presentation and not just a fancy closing *'tacked on'* for effect.

Mark shared some thoughts on audience retention too. He said, *"raw is real,"* in that we shouldn't sanitize our material or try to make it too perfect. Makes sense to reach an audience by being ourselves. He mentioned that *"less is more"* in that we tend to put too much into our presentations. *I've found myself doing that on occasion. But it is an area that I am aware of and am still working to make sure I allow the real Bob out so my audiences can see and experience what I really believe.*

Mark talked about timing, too. **FEAR – false endings appearing real.** Have you ever been listening to a speaker and thought they were closing, only to find they still had lots to say? How did you feel? Don't do that to your audiences. When it's time to close, do so and do it with impact. Don't fool your audiences – go for the close and finish on time.

One of the most effective things Mark did was share what he called the Lincoln insight. Here is what I recall him sharing with us.

Seems, President Lincoln had a political adversary who was a 'church going' man. To avoid controversy President Lincoln would often sneak into services after they started and leave just before they finished.

One Sunday, as President Lincoln was leaving, he was approached by a Presidential aide who asked him if he enjoyed the sermon. His reply was, "It was well crafted and delivered." His aide pursued the matter and asked again, "So you liked the sermon?"

Irritated, Lincoln replied, "No son, I did not!" Confused, the aide stammered, "Buuuut, you said it was well crafted and delivered?"

Lincoln went on to explain, "It was well crafted and delivered, but the preacher failed in one thing." "What was that?" the aide asked.

Lincoln replied, **"He didn't challenge us to do anything GREAT with what he shared - in that he failed."**

52

Mark's story caught my attention! I committed to making sure I don't make the same mistake when I speak. Mark asked us some questions that are worth asking you to think about as well:

- Are your closings a culmination **or** simply a stopping point?

- What one thing could you do to make your presentation more of an experience? *(Esthetics, escapism, education, entertainment?)*

- What impression are you trying to leave **after** your speech? Why?

- What are the 2-3 most important values that drive your life? Do they show up in your presentations? How? *(This was one of the major shifts for me.)*

- What great thing are you asking listeners to do when you close?

Your thoughts and answers on these questions will give you a better insight into who you are and what you need to share to be effective as a speaker. **And, isn't that what you really want?**

Ask yourself,
"If I had only sixty seconds on the stage, what
would I absolutely have to say to get my
message across?"
Jeff Dewar

Class notes

This section draws from slides used in my various on-site or live classes. I expound and expand on elements from each one, based on my own experience and application. On site, I spend time, sharing my own stories and on-stage lessons to help my students grasp and built on these ideas. This made this course a favorite at several colleges in the Vancouver area for the 6 or so years where I taught.

In fact one college voted me the **'most marketable instructor'** and gave me a nice plaque. Their sales staff often used my series of presentation skills classes as a selling or closing point when enrolling new students. Being they were on commission, I found this interesting. ☺

I've drawn these **'class notes'** from many sources: books I've studied, notes taken, in depth conversations and Q&A sessions with fellow professionals, my Toastmasters experience, and my own experiences on the platform over the past 16 plus years.

Make a point of personalizing or internalizing them to your own specific situation and needs. Use the ones that apply to the type of presentation and style you've chosen.

Touching on the basics

Speaker Dorothy Leeds, best-selling author of **"POWER SPEAK"** has built a very successful career working with people by helping them be more effective as presenters. Dorothy discovered that the majority of her clients and struggling speakers had a pattern of flaws leading to ineffective speaking.

These **six major faults** in speaking often separate the *successful* speaker from the *mediocre* speaker. In our live classes this section is prefaced with a story of growing up in California and living close to a fault line; a fault line that made the ground less stable and more susceptible to earthquakes. When you craft your presentation make sure you build on solid foundations.

Give some thought to each of the six speaking faults. Have you seen it in your own presentations? Have you seen it in the efforts of others?

How would you avoid this fault or minimize it in your own speaking?

- **An unclear purpose**
- **Lack of clear organization and leadership**
- **Too much information or data**
- **Not enough support for your ideas, concepts, or information**
- **Monotonous voice or sloppy speech habits**
- **Not meeting the real needs of the audience**

Keep in mind, challenging each of these speaking 'faults' face-on is an opportunity to grow as a speaker. There is not one fault listed here that cannot be overcome or minimized in your striving to be a better speaker.

"Miracles' occur when students apply their efforts and focus to replacing these faults with strong foundations; and in practicing until those foundations are strong enough to support them effectively. **You can too!**

Platform professional, **Ira M. Hayes** shared a number of focus points he considered necessary to successful presentations. I frequently share these with my students as the '**SEVEN BE-ATTITUDES**' of Effective Speaking.

1. **BE** - informative
2. **BE** - valuable
3. **BE** - interesting
4. **BE** - memorable
5. **BE** - believable
6. Strive to **BE** - inspirational
7. **BE** - enjoyable!

Give some thought on how to best incorporate these **be-attitudes** into your presentations. When you apply some new attitudes, you often get some new responses from your audiences.

Speaking professional **Ty Boyd,** from Charlotte, NC had **ten points or building blocks for success** he felt you needed to be effective as a communicator. Based on his long and successful run as a professional speaker, I took note! His lessons live on in those of us who apply them in our careers. Thanks Ty! When he spoke at NSA in Orlando a couple of years back, at 80 years old, he still had it!

1. **FIRE** in your belly
2. Have **FOCUS**
3. Good speakers **PERFORM**
4. Use **COLOR** in your voice, your body, and your energy
5. Use your face – **SMILE!**
6. Use the rest of your **BODY** too (be aware of body language)
7. Learn to effectively use your **EYES**
8. Maintain physical **BALANCE**
9. **INVOLVE** your audience
10. **PRACTICE, practice, practice!**

One of the biggest misconceptions of public speaking I've encountered over the years is people's persistence in separating platform style presentations from one-to-one meeting or smaller group presentations.

Often this is simply a matter of perception, **"Oh my, I have to give a presentation!"** People in business – powerful people – have learned to harness the power of speaking whenever and wherever they are communicating verbally. You can too, using some of the tips and techniques outlined in this book.

One question I frequently get from my clients and students is **"how do you give your presentations without notes?"** A good question! Sometimes I do use notes. I don't have a problem with having someone using them, as long as they are unobtrusive and don't take audience focus away from your presentation. There are several famous speakers who effectively use notes in their presentations.

Using notes as a back-up to give you a sense of confidence is okay. So is using notes as reference or to quote a specific fact or quotation. Keep them simple and don't get in the habit of depending on them or obviously refer to them during your presentation.

One exercise shared with my students was to ask them to hold up and look at their hand. **"What do you see?"** They usually say, **"A thumb and four fingers,"** which is of course, the obvious answer.

My answer to that same question is **"A presentation, without notes, up to 20 minutes."** I see an opening, three points and a conclusion.

I can remember 5 points or 5 things! Can't you? When we keep it simple and focus on the main points it makes it easier to remember.

Using gestures

Here are a few ideas on using gestures to add movement and energy to your presentation.

- **Use gestures** to channel your nervous muscle tension by carefully selecting or choreographing body movements that emphasize specific speech points. Nervous energy can effectively be used to lend welcome animation to your movements and presentation.

- Using **gestures** effectively is a whole area of its own, but a few points must be made here. Audiences will believe what they see in your face, manners and body movement long BEFORE they believe what you say.

Gestures can amplify your speech by including facial expressions and body language to illustrate pain, pleasure, sarcasm, sincerity, enthusiasm, or disinterest, as well as other emotions.

Here are a few more story starters for you. Use them to kick start your brain or perhaps as the basis for a story to include in one of your speeches.

TIPS as a foundation for a story:

- The number 1 principle for success _____ :
- 2 ways of approaching _____ :
- 3 questions to ask when _____ :
- 4 cornerstones of _____ :
- 5 key elements of _____ :
- 6 steps to creating a _____ :
- 7 ways to _____ :
- 8 secrets of _____ :
- 9 lies or myths in the _____ :
- 10 tips when using _____ :

Ten Commandments of informative presentations

Here are a few comments on tips gleaned from ideas shared by my friend Marjorie Brody, CSP, CPAE on how to be more effective when presenting.

- **Less is more:** Avoid the mistake of the amateur speaker and resist the urge to give them everything you've researched about your topic. Share only the relevant points and information needed to get your message across and call them to action.

- **It's a *'jungle'* to the audience:** They don't always see the whole or BIG picture. Part of your role as the informative speaker is to be their *guide* and direct their path; to cut a *clear* path that they can follow.

- **Assume they don't understand:** This is where many amateur speakers fail by assuming their audiences understand the words and the concepts they share. Start with the lowest denominator and build or expand on their current understanding. Then skillfully move them along the path to where you are.

- **Keep relating back to what they already know:** This allows people to assimilate and start mentally comparing what you are saying to what they know. This allows them to see where it might apply to them and acts as a springboard to getting them to accept and act on the information you share. Metaphors work well in this respect.

- **Use visuals and simplify:** Many people *get it* better when they can *see it!* Using visuals allows you to augment your words and helps keep it simple. Share only enough information to give them the sense and the direction you want.

- **Keep lingo and jargon to a minimum: Please!!!!** Stay away from shoptalk and business or industry buzzwords. There will be people in your audience who will not know them and will be mentally left at the starting gate. Our role as presenters is to bridge the gap and share knowledge, not erect barriers.

- **Insist on their interaction:** When people are involved and interact, it facilitates growth and allows them to take in the information. It helps in the retention and follow-up action after you finish.

- **Demonstrate:** '*Show*' them is always better than '*tell*' them! What they see and experience they more successfully retain.

- **Do the unexpected:** This is where your *creative* side is called into play. What do you need to do to get their attention, keep it, and motivate them to actually do something with what you are outlining?

- **Sell:** Even though you are sharing information, you still have to sell it. What are they going to do with it, when, and why? If you don't sell it, they will not apply it.

In addition to being a very delightful person, Marjorie is a commiserate professional on the platform and one of the most successful entrepreneurs in this field I have ever met.

Give some thought to the points she taught me as you structure and prepare your session. These tips work – very well!

 **Another set of stories starters for your use.** These take a different approach in sharing warnings or cautions that might be of interest to your prospective audiences.

Warning or cautions as a basis for stories:

- The single biggest fallacy of _____:
- 2 dangers of _____:
- 3 wrong turns made by _____:
- 4 common mistakes of _____:
- The 5 myths of _____:
- 6 major obstacles in _____:
- 7 deadly sins in _____:
- 8 roadblocks to _____:
- 9 detours in _____:
- 10 ways to waste _____:

10 success guides
for effective business presentations

These tips work just as well on stage as they do in the boardroom or in front of a client. Presentations are more successful when prepared and presented with a clear focus. We teach these same points when working with sales people who depend on their ability to present and persuade to make a living. We help sales people become sales leaders – and applying these points is one of the ways they succeed. Use them to be more effective when you are presenting your ideas.

- **Keep it short:** Time is precious and more so as you move up the leadership chain. Value their time and keep it simple, short, and to the point. Focus and deliver solid value in the time allotted.
- **Know your audience:** Do your homework in advance so you can tailor or customize your presentation (sales, informative, interview, etc.) to your audience and get and keep their interest.
- **Use visuals to add interest:** Pictures, props, and visuals help your audience get the point or reinforce your message in a shorter period of time.
- **Get them involved:** Audience involvement and interaction is essential in this very competitive arena. If you have figures to be worked out, ask them to do so. Remember, if it is their data, they trust it and give it more credibility.
- **Start and end on time!** I can't emphasize this one enough. If you ask for 15 minutes of someone's time you'd better be closing your mouth and your briefcase on or before the 15-minute mark. If you are given 45 minutes to make a presentation, make sure you are done at or before the 45 minute mark. This is what separates the professionals from the mediocre performers.

I have never had a client complain that I finished a minute or so ahead of schedule. I have seen many speakers lose credibility when they went over their time and made the meeting run late. Good lesson – finish one time!

- **Dress appropriately:** Dress for Success – not excess! Make a point of understanding the dress code for the group or situation.
  One suggestion would be to always be **slightly** better dressed than the best dressed person in attendance.
- **Use short sentences, simple phrases:** Make it easy for the audience to gain acceptance and understanding of your concepts. Don't assume that they are fully literate – keep in mind most of the morning newspapers *(read by many executives)* are written to grade 6-8 reading levels.
- **Avoid humor unless appropriate:** Effective use of humor can be a great bridge. However, you can blow yourself out of the running by using something that offends someone in the audience. They may not even tell you, but they won't buy from you or deal with you.
- **Distribute handouts at the end of your presentation:** This idea applies to any use of handouts. Unless you need to have them refer to them, use them as a tool, or write something in them during your presentation – leave them for the end. People tend to read what you've given them instead of listening to you.
- **Don't bluff. If you don't know, find out!** Your credibility is a fragile thing in the business arena. Do your homework so you have the basics at your fingertips. Don't try to wing it or fake it when asked a question outside that parameter. Make sure you understand the question and make a specific commitment to find out and get back to them. Then do so!

If your career or success depends on your ability to persuade an audience or buyer, these tips will help you understand how to structure your presentation for maximum effect.

Business leaders are busy and you need to be clear and concise to win and keep their attention. Unless you know them, start strong, present value, and conclude with impact.

Your career, and your success in your business and your community has a direct relationship to your effectiveness in working with people – your superiors, your staff, your suppliers, your co-workers, and most especially your clients. Doesn't it make sense to invest the effort to ensure you have the best opportunity to succeed?

A 12 step process
for building a good presentation

This is almost self-explanatory as a guideline in preparing for a presentation. The secret is in being systematic and building toward your goal of constructing a successful presentation.

Use this format or the other examples as methods to help gather your thoughts, organize them in a relevant and orderly manner, and then deliver them with passion to persuade your audience to accept and act on them.

- **Select the Topic**
- **Limit the Topic to One Central Theme** *(what is the most important goal)*
- **Gather the Information**
- **Choose a Method of Organization (see examples pages 82-83)**
- **Outline Your Main Points**
- **Collect Supporting Data**
- **Check for Accuracy**
- **Design the Introduction**
- **Write a Strong Conclusion**
- **Put Together a Final Draft**
- **Practice Your Presentation**
- **Practice, Practice, Practice**
- **Confidently deliver it with passion and power!**

Following this simple 12-step process will help you take the journey from idea to implementation in front of an audience. It works because it is systematic and helps you create a logical flow for your presentation.

Five Steps to persuasion
...key to successful presentations

In essence, every presentation aims to persuade an audience. We seek to persuade them to listen and perhaps agree with what we present. Crafting our thoughts with this in mind is what proves our professionalism.

- **Get their attention:** If you don't capture my attention, you'll never gain my acceptance or my action on your behalf. What does it take to do that? Do it!

- **Demonstrate their need to know:** This is where you help me see the relevance of what you are about to share. If I don't see a need in my life, career, or company I will not respond favorably to your call to action and you are wasting both of our time.

- **Satisfy that need:** This is where you outline the solutions in ways that I can apply and benefit.

- **Visualize the results:** Help me see the *finished* results; the changes as outlined in your solution. Give me a *mental* picture of my need being met and my satisfaction attained and I will be more receptive to act or buy.

- **Request their action:** This is where many mediocre sales people blow it. **Ask for the order**. Call me to action! Challenge me to do something great!

This is a brief summary of the steps behind persuasion. Keep them in mind as you structure your presentation. Keep in mind what the audience reaction will be to each area. Selling your ideas as a presenter is very similar to what profession sales people do with their clients and the process follows a similar path.

Using humor
...a few safety tips

In the professional speakers world there is a saying in response to the question, **"Do you have to be funny?" "Only, if you want to be paid!"**

While that is not entirely true, humor, when properly used, does make your presentation more interesting and helps build bridges with your audience.

Here are a few tips to remember if you plan on including relevant humor:

- Punch lines? Remember them!!!! Practice until you can nail it if awoken from a dead sleep.
- Ensure the anecdote is appropriate and relates to your presentation – not just inserted for the laughs. Too many amateurs undermine their efforts when they insert something fun that doesn't relate to their audiences.
- Timing is everything – practice it! A lot!!!
- BE KIND! Don't pick on any group or person. Pick on yourself! This also helps build bridges with your audience by showing you are a real person.
- Vulgarity and sexist remarks are NOT allowed. They always work against you.
- Humor doesn't travel well. Make sure it works in different locations. Humor doesn't always translate to other cultures.

While speaking in Tehran, Iran (2009) I shared a story that always got a laugh in North America. Nothing! No laughter, no chuckles, nothing. I asked the translator about it and he said, "I didn't get it!" Once I explained it to him, he laughed.

Later that week we used it again in Kish; and we got laughs, lots of laughs. He helped me bridge the cultural laughter wall.

Using visual aids effectively

In the past few years, there has been a backlash to visuals like PowerPoint, primarily because they have been overdone and detract from the presentation. Too many speakers stumble through presentations using visuals as crutches not catch points to reinforce their message.

Many speakers are staying away from using them or use them sparingly. *I actually recall a meeting planner saying, "Thank you," when told I wasn't going to use PowerPoint with her group.*

If you are going to use visuals, use them well to support and reinforce the message you intend to share with your audience. Here are a few tips on their effective use.

- **Test for clarity:** Can they be clearly understood by the audience?
- **Make them relevant to the presentation:** Use only the ones that will reinforce or make your presentation stronger and more memorable. If they don't relate to the audience or the topic – dump them!
- **Use sparingly:** Professionals use only enough to get the job done or to visually illustrate a point. Remember they aren't there to see a slide show, but to listen to what you have to say.
- **Keep them simple:** Don't overdo it… and please don't use every aid in the book or all of the bells and whistles *(PowerPoint has been overdone to death!)*
- **Keep them short:** Rule of thumb 6 words per line and a maximum of 6 lines on any slide. Less is more in this case. Remember they are there as a guide or reinforcement not a stand-alone learning piece.
- **DON'T read your slides:** If all your information is on your slides and you are merely reading them, why do you need to be there?
- **Pictures:** Often the best slides are those which are more visual to help the audience see or experience something. Adding a few words may help to clarify what they are seeing, but keep it short.
- **Don't show prematurely:** Practice with them so they come up only as needed and are taken off just as quickly.
- **Show only when referring to them:** They are there to **reinforce** or illustrate your presentation. They should only be there when you are

referring to them. Don't be afraid to build in blanks or know how to go to blank screen (Ctl B) or white screen (Ctl W) when needed.

- **Make direct reference to them:** This is one time where it is occasionally good to turn and look at a visual for a moment. This helps draw the audience's eyes accordingly.
- **Don't talk to visual aids – talk to us:** Having said that, don't talk while your back is turned to the audience. Look, turn back, and talk to your audience!
- **Maintain them in good order:** Just like shining your shoes and pressing your clothes, keep your visuals in good working order. If they get frayed, worn, or outdated, replace them.

If you are planning to use visuals, plan to use them well. Understand they are there to reinforce what you have to say and keep them clear, concise, and relevant to your presentation. If you are using them, make sure they are a value-added accessory – not a distraction.

Answering audience questions

There are times when taking questions from your audience can enhance your chances of getting your message across as well as help your audience learn by being more interactive. Here are a few tips to help in that regard:

- **Announce the Q&A session period in advance:** If you are going to incorporate this into your presentation, let your audience know early. Then make sure you structure your presentation to allow enough time for Q&A.
- **Don't evaluate questions:** You aren't there to judge or evaluate – but to share answers and help them clarify or amplify what you've just said.
- **Answer pleasantly and politely:** If you get ruffled or take questions as a personal challenge it will show. This will undermine your credibility faster than anything I have seen. So be cool **or** don't open yourself up to be challenged.
- **Use paralanguage** *(voice and body)* **to respond to questions:** *'Let me see if I understand you correctly?"* Clarify and respond to show them you listened and value their input. This is also where you can state or restate the question to ensure the rest of the audience or the audience on tape hears it prior to the answer being given.

- **Look at audience when you answer:** This is one time where looking directly at the person who asked you the question is a good thing. Respect them and answer them directly.
- **Admit to not knowing ALL the answers:** We don't have to be the expert on everything. Make sure you understand what they are asking and make a commitment to get back to them with the answer. Then do it!
- **Ask for audience help** *(when necessary)*: This can be a good model even when you know the answer. Let other people be the heroes and share the stage. It works wonders in making the session a shared and memorable one.

Question periods can be a **wonderful way to involve your audience** and add additional points not already covered in your presentation. Additionally, they allow you to develop and share additional material from your wealth of knowledge. Have a few questions to prime the pump if necessary. *"One of the more frequent questions I get is…"* or *"The other day someone asked me…."* It works!

One final tip: **Never end on a Q&A session**. Always have a few closing comments or a story to finish and allow the audience to experience the end of your presentation on a high point. Nothing is lamer than asking and not getting any questions and following that embarrassing silence, closing on that experience.

"A theme is a memory aid; it helps you through the presentation just as it also provides the thread of continuity for your audience."
Dave Carey

Moving upward

"the top predictor of success and upward mobility, professionally, is how much you enjoy public speaking and how effective you are at it!"

Stanford University Survey for AT&T

"As soon as you move one step up from the bottom, your effectiveness depends on your ability to reach others through the spoken or written word."

Peter Drucker - Author

"Effective speaking skills are an essential foundation for success in any endeavor. Professionally or personally, it is one of the most important skills you'll ever acquire! And it is easily acquired!"

**Bob 'idea Man' Hooey
Accredited Speaker
Presentations Skills Success Coach**

Getting your competitive edge

When I joined Toastmasters, my mentor, Gary Harper told me about the value of competition. He said, *"Hooey, if you want to get good, get into competition."*

There are reasons why competition can be a success tool in honing your skills and moving them to another level. One of course, would be that competition itself will pull something *extra* out of you. The stretch of being competitive can be a benefit in itself.

The other benefit is the potential of winning and getting the opportunity to hone a speech through up to 4 levels of competition in Toastmasters (Club, Area, Division, and District). Each time your presentation gets tighter, more focused, and perhaps even funnier.

 I had the privilege coaching Calgarian, Rowena Romero to the 2005 TI World Championships in Toronto, Ontario. She was diligent in working and fine tuning her speech. We went through countless re-writes, phone calls, and two trips to Calgary to see and coach on-site before she was satisfied and ready to take it to Toronto. I was so impressed by her commitment to giving her best and to allowing me to creatively work with her. She was a joy to coach.

Rowena's kind words to me: *"YOU were part of that performance for me. Working with you last year provided a good training ground for me to fully utilize facial, hand, and body gestures. I always used these aspects before, but not to the level that I am now. Many people commented on how I "commanded the stage" or that I "owned the stage" – that I didn't just deliver a speech, I brought the scene to life. The audience felt like they were in the car with me looking at Naked Guy or that they were Officer Kowalchuk. (Characters in Rowena's speech.)*

I gained the confidence of "striking a pose" and not having to say a word. Before, I would have wanted to continue talking through every motion. (Show it - don't tell it!) However, this truly became "actions speak louder than words" – everything from posing like Naked Guy, to the head going side-to-side for the windshield wipers, to the blinking hands for the hazard lights. I felt confident enough to just let the "physical" do the "talking" for me. Thank you for the training!" **I was humbled by her words!**

That brings me to my real point. When competing, it is important to maintain your focus on *giving* the audience something of value. Your *primary* job as a speaker is to deliver your best possible presentation (that day).

Hint: Each time you present, you are competing with your last performance. This applies in non-competitive presentations as well. In business and sales you are competing with other people to earn the respect and business of your clients. You are also competing with your last sales conversation.

A presentation should be structured and directed to *giving* definite benefits to those in the audience. The judge's job is to listen to each speaker and pick the top three presentations. Competitors lose when they attempt to do the judges job.

As I reminded Rowena (*and remind myself each time I speak*), trust the process, do your homework, and know there is someone in the audience who needs to hear what you have to say. **Speak to that person**, even though you may never know who they are, or how you helped them. That is the win and that is what motivates me.

Our *real* competition is *within* ourselves. Are you better today than you were the last time you spoke? Did the value you bring to the stage increase? The *competitive edge* is in pushing yourself to be better than you've ever been before.

Enjoy the competitions in your life and in speaking. But remember, the real prize is winning the hearts and minds of your audience.

When Speaking for Success – **speak to win… their hearts and minds.**

"It takes one hour of preparation for each minute of presentation time."
Wayne Burgraff

Sometimes more… invest it well to deliver it better!

Effective communication is really a part of the 'sales' and management process

People buy, agree, or say *'yes'* to something, for emotional reasons in relation to benefits 'perceived' and sometimes received. They often use facts to back up or justify their purchase or decision.

- This also applies in leading teams and generating buy-in for programs, policies, or goals.
- It applies to being a successful salesperson.
- It applies, as well, to being successful in making a presentation.

In your communication, it would be wise to keep in mind that people will react *'emotionally'* to what you say or write. You are *'selling'* your ideas, your position, your services, your products, and most importantly *yourself* whenever you communicate.

Perhaps it would be beneficial to take a moment and discuss the basic reasons we've found that people buy into or say 'yes' to something. These emotional needs underlie the reason they buy into your programs, buy your products, or buy you as a person to work with, follow, or deal with; why they can be persuaded to say 'yes' to something. They also provide guidance as you craft a presentation.

Psychologist Abraham Maslow did exhaustive research and concluded that all people had a hierarchy of needs. He ranked them from the most basic to the loftiest: **physiological (sheer survival), security, social, self-esteem, and self-actualization.**

Remember, when you communicate effectively, people want to be involved in your life, your projects, and in helping you succeed. Effective leadership is focused on pulling diverse talents, skills, needs, and drives of your team into common goals and to focusing their energies to succeed.

These insights on emotional needs can help you design and deliver powerful a presentation.

Emotional needs:

1. To make money
2. To save money
3. To save time
4. To avoid effort
5. To gain comfort
6. To improve health
7. To escape pain
8. To be popular
9. To attract the opposite sex
10. To gain praise
11. To conserve our possessions
12. To increase our enjoyment
13. To satisfy curiosity
14. To protect our family
15. To be in style
16. To satisfy an appetite
17. To emulate others
18. To have beautiful things
19. To avoid criticism
20. To avoid trouble
21. To take advantage of opportunities
22. To be individual and unique
23. To protect our reputation
24. To gain control over aspects of our lives
25. To be safe

Whether you are talking one-on-one, presenting to a group of people, or communicating in writing, your audience, team, or readers will be evaluating and reacting to your words and *'filtering'* them through one or more of the above emotional needs.

Tough sell isn't it? But if you have done your homework and researched the needs, background, and thought processes of those you want to reach, it will be much easier. You can enhance your chances of success by carefully crafting your communication to touch or draw on the emotional needs of your audience, team, or readership. Be cautious in its use.

Some would ask, isn't this manipulation? My gut reaction would be to say no! On the surface it might appear that way, but only you know your *'true'* motives.

If your *'true'* motive is to communicate more clearly, more effectively; and your desire is to serve them by giving them all the relevant information they need in a way that makes it easier for them to relate to it – then I say go for it! Having an honest desire to help people is what builds a foundation for success under your career or business and helps ensure both longevity and success. That is one of the key secrets to Speaking for Success.

This applies to working with family and friends, as well as clients, co-workers, management, and staff. So, remember, communication, especially effective communication, is really a process of selling – selling your ideas, your desires, your dreams, and your future. How effective will you be in persuading people to buy in? How successful will you be in inspiring them to help you?

The Gettysburg Address by Abraham Lincoln was short and historically impactful in an effort to bring the nation back together. It was powerful in its simplicity and its structure. Take a moment to read this, perhaps out loud, and enjoy its power. Then use its inspiration as you work to craft your own.

"Fourscore and seven years ago our fathers brought forth on this continent a new nation, conceived in liberty and dedicated to the proposition that all men are created equal.

Now we are engaged in a great civil war, testing whether that nation or any nation so conceived and so dedicated can long endure. We are met on a great battlefield of that war.

We have come to dedicate a portion of that field as a final resting-place for those who here gave their lives that that nation might live. It is altogether fitting and proper that we should do this.

But in a larger sense, we cannot dedicate, we cannot consecrate, we cannot hallow this ground. The brave men, living and dead who struggled here have consecrated it far above our poor power to add or detract.

The world will little note nor long remember what we say here, but it can never forget what they did here. It is for us the living rather to be dedicated here to the unfinished work which they who fought here have thus far so nobly advanced.

*It is rather for us to be here dedicated to the great task remaining before us - that from these honoured dead we take increased devotion to that cause for which they gave the last full measure of devotion - that we here highly resolve that these dead shall not have died in vain, that this nation under God shall have a new birth freedom, and **that government of the people, by the people, for the people shall not perish from the earth.**"*

Descriptive stories sell on more than one level

If you know anything about business or sales, perhaps you've heard taught that communicating **Features, Advantages,** and **Benefits (FAB)** is a more effective approach than just feature dumping on our prospective customers. **It is!**

- But, how effectively do we incorporate that in our sales conversations?
- How effectively do we incorporate it in our presentations or communication?

Let me share a simple experience where a young shoe salesman (Joseph) did this very well as he presented his product. We all need shoes and, hopefully, since we are on our feet a lot, we select some that are comfortable, yet stylish to wear when we are at work. *At least that is my story.* ☺

Feature	/ **Advantage** (which means)	/ **Benefit** (to customer)
Calfskin leather	/ molds to your foot	/ custom made feel
Full leather lining	/ finished feel	/ instant comfort
Traditional loafer	/ will stay in style	/ wear for years

I was in Puerto Vallarta doing some sailing one summer. One afternoon I was enjoying a quiet break doing some window shopping. A very stylish, yet simple, pair of two-tone loafers caught my eye in a little shoe store off the quaint cobblestone street. Thinking I was only looking, I stepped into the store to check them out. I picked them up and quickly put them down. My initial reaction was, *"Wow... these are not cheap, even for here!"*

My young and *very wise* shoe expert approached and engaged me in conversation about my visit to his store, to Puerto Vallarta, and what I did for a living. I made the mistake of telling him I was a professional speaker and sales success trainer who traveled sharing ideas on how others could be more successful in their lives, careers, sales, etc. (Guess he figured I could really afford them. ☺)

Picking up the shoes and holding them with care, he said, *"You know, when you wear these traditional loafers, you're going to have a big smile on your face because* **'one of the great things'** *about these shoes is they're soft calfskin leather with a full leather lining. And as you wear them, they will mold to the shape of your feet, giving you a custom-made feel."*

He continued, *"It would be fun to walk around in custom-made shoes, don't you think?"* I hesitantly agreed, *"…it would be great."*

He could have just said, *"These shoes are all leather, which is flexible, making them very comfortable."* On the surface that sounds good, doesn't it? However what he said *engaged* me and was much more effective in getting me to seriously consider investing in a pair for myself, don't you think?

He talked about how the shoes were made. He mentioned, they were bench-crafted, which meant **one** person was completely responsible for making **this specific pair** of shoes.

Joseph then went in for the kill, *"Since they are bench-crafted, they have the artisan's name on them. When they're finished, these shoes have no nicks, no scratches, and all of the components fit perfectly. Unlike shoes made on an assembly line, these shoes are* **one of a kind**.*"*

Then he asked me a simple closing question, *"What size do you wear?"* He then proceeded to have me try on a pair in my size; just to see how they felt.

Long story, made short:
He was right, they are delightful to wear. When I walked out of his store, both of us had big smiles on our faces. I could hardly wait for the snow to leave so I could take them out for a walk in Northern Alberta.

Simple story of how one young salesman took his craft to the next level by engaging his client (audience) and telling a story that allowed me to see myself in those shoes.

- Do you do that with your clients when they come into your store?
- Or when you visit them in their place of business?
- Do you do this when you speak to your audience?

For example:

Do you know enough about your ideas and products that you can craft engaging stories to help your customers (audience) see themselves sitting in front of that big screen Plasma TV, on that leather sofa with matching love seat and chair, end tables, coordinated lamps and accents to enjoy that quiet evening together?

- Can they see themselves enjoying their well-funded retirement?
- Can they see themselves driving that navy blue, sporty new Mustang convertible?

You get the point!

Are you willing to engage your clients (audience) to help them see it in their mind's eye before they see it in their house, office, or life? Do you know enough about the benefits your services provide that you can create captivating stories that help your prospective clients see themselves enjoying the benefit of wisely selecting you to help enhance their lives, businesses, and careers?

- Do you think this might help you build and expand your business or enhance your career?
- Do you think you can craft your presentation successfully to help your audience accept and act on your message?

Get walking and talking on your journey to **Speaking for Success** and in selling your message.

"I learned this, at least, by my experiment: that if one advances confidently in the direction of his dreams, and endeavors to live the life which he had imagined, he will meet with a success unexpected in common hours."
Henry David Thoreau
Walden, or Life in the Woods

Crafting your message – The "IT" method

People often ask how I create and develop my topics and presentations. They want to know how I am able to skillfully infuse creativity into each one. Being Canada's 'Idea Man' helps. ☺

One of the methods is the "**IT**" **Method** which is a creativity exercise to help you **develop, organize, and dynamically deliver the content** of your presentation. In computer jargon 'I.T.' *usually* indicates information technology. In that same sense, when you are speaking, you are *essentially* imparting or transmitting specific knowledge, expertise, experience, or information.

Let's use that same acronym to help build the components of your successful presentation.

The IT! Method, as envisioned, has five basic components or sequences to follow.

- **Thunder Think™ IT!** *(Creative thinking by Bob 'Idea Man' Hooey)*
- **Re-group IT!**
- **Fine-Tune IT!**
- **Spice IT up!**
- **Do IT!**

Thunder Think IT!

This is your chance to brainstorm: capture ideas, concepts, and information. Brainstorming is a method for developing creative solutions to problems. Your goal here is to think freely, putting everything that you may want to say down on paper or on your screen. You can *brainstorm* or *thunder-think* on your own; but often a small group brainstorming together can really augment this creative process.

Over the years I have found the **power of leveraged brainpower** to be an effective tool in problem solving, business planning and development, and in creating customized, effective presentations for my various audiences. I frequently use a brainstorming method to create and design my presentations. Even when I have presented the topic numerous times, following this path allows me to remain fresh and create something specifically designed for each client.

Yellow-sticky notes, such as Post-its™, can give the creative process great fertility and flexibility. You can brainstorm more freely when not hampered by a linear outline or a sequentially generated form or structure. You can do this in a mind mapping format, but this works well from a visual and has a built in flexibility factor.

With your primary topic or presentation theme identified, and the yellow-sticky notes in hand, capture any and all:

- **Ideas**
- **Facts**
- **Related stories**
- **Examples**
- **Jokes or funny connections**
- **Personal experiences**
- **Miscellaneous**

Yellow-sticky everything and anything that relates to your subject, perhaps *flavored* by the particular audience. Don't be concerned about relating all of your ideas or whether you even plan to use all of the generated ideas. Just capture all of the ideas – one per yellow-sticky! Collect the ideas and stick ALL of them on a flipchart or a nearby blank wall or picture window.

Try to keep your left-brain (*your internal editor*) out of this brainstorming process. This activity is strictly a right-brain function – pure free association, idea generation. **HAVE FUN!**

TIP: Brainstorming works best when a time limit is established.

Re-group IT!
Now step back mentally from this sea of yellow sticky notes and do what you might naturally do – put the notes in groups or clusters!

Group your ideas on the notes according to the natural associations you observe in the evolving material. Do not try to *force* every idea into a category; some will be left over. If you've ever done Mind Mapping, this is a very similar in process. What parts (*notes*) relate to each other and form natural groups or clusters?

I actually use this method when I am assembling publications like this one where I am drawing on two workbooks to create this updated book version just for you.

TIP: If you find that a category has more than 10 notes, consider whether it should really be more than one category!

After you group the sticky notes, give each group a *working* name or title. Next, ask yourself the question: "Given this *particular* audience, which of these groups do I want them to hear about first, in the body of the presentation, second, third," and so on. Try to keep the number of groups relatively small. Many people believe that three to five is the ideal number of points around which to organize your presentation. This is not an absolute! Just try to keep it simple.

Save the unused groups. They may provide input for other parts of the presentation. These groups also can provide a source for the question-and-answer period of the presentation and may be used in future presentations on the same subject to other audiences. They can form the foundation for additional presentations or articles.

Look at all of the sticky notes generated from the brainstorming and see what categories or groups you can come up with. Write these in large circles on the flipchart.

Fine-Tune IT!
Applying sound *simplicity* principles, trim the ideas within each group and put them into a logical order or sequence. Remember, even though many experts believe three is the ideal number, you are not bound to it.

Go back to your presentation strategy and review your position, desired actions, and listener benefits. Make sure you define these items in your presentation. Usually, the desired actions and listener benefits should be stated and restated in the introduction and in the conclusion.

Spice IT up!

You are now ready to add some 'spice' to your presentation framework! The purpose of spice is to add *memor-ability*, en-liven, aid retention, and otherwise provide interesting relief and reinforcement of your program or message. Use it wisely – but use it!

Spice it all! Don't forget to spice the beginning and the ending or conclusion. Remember the opening and the closing thoughts or statements are the most important items in the presentation. These items are the most likely to be 'remembered' by your audiences. Identify where the *peaks* and *valleys* of the presentation are and what type of spice could be added to the *new* or *improved* presentation.

Here are ideas to make your speech a bit more appealing to your audiences. These ingredients are the contents of your own **"Spice Cupboard:"**

- **Stories** – that conveys emotion and grabs their attention and encapsulates the lessons. Make sure to use your own stories. If you share something from another source, credit it!
- **Quotes** – that reinforce or remind them of your message can be sprinkled throughout your speech.
- **Facts** – to substantiate or reinforce your credibility on the platform are always a welcome addition.
- **Props** – that help visually illustrate or command attention.
- **Costumes** – if they enhance your presentation and illustrate your point. Choose wisely! ☺ *I remember, and so did my audience, walking on stage at our CAPS convention in Vancouver. I did so, at 7AM in my pj's to illustrate a point. Even though this occurred 10 years ago, I still get comments. Hmmm!*
- **Handouts** – that give solid value and follow up information or resources or are an interactive part of the session. Most professionals call them learning guides or resource guides which helps us reinforce their value.
- **Audio** – sound bites and back-ground music to assist in the lesson or setting moods.
- **Video** – illustrate a point; introduce another concept or expert into the mix. YouTube has provided some invaluable visuals for presentations. Use selectively and make sure they are relevant to your program or presentation.
- **Slides** – overheads or PowerPoint™ that are used as a tool to reinforce, remind, or help the audience visualize something you as the speaker are saying.

Anything you use from your 'Spice Cupboard' is *only* there to support and make what you say more impactful, easier to understand, or more memorable. **If it overshadows you as the speaker – reduce its use or eliminate it entirely.**

The audience wants to hear and see you, not a *slick* slide show.

Do IT!
Now that all of the planning work has been done, the presenter must write, and edit, edit, edit before developing the visuals or other aids to accompany the presentation.

Building the foundation and organization or structure using the IT method is the start. To bring your presentation to fruition and effectively present IT takes additional thought and polishing as you flesh IT out and prepare IT in its final form. **Good luck in your quest.**

On the following two pages, I have included two examples of speech outlines for your information.

- **The first is a linear outline, similar to what we were taught in school.**

I've blocked it out so you can write in your answers in the appropriate places. Then, as you fine tune your presentation, you can add, subtract or edit your thoughts. This can be an effective tool in helping you think through the flow of ideas and structure in your speech.

- **The second is a sample of a modified creative mind map styled speech organization tool.**

This is more along the method I use and dovetails nicely with the ideas expressed in Crafting the IT way. It allows you to let your mind flow and generate ideas.

Capture the ideas and then group them into clusters or natural connections. I simply restructure the clusters into a natural flow which becomes my speech outline and path. Feel free to copy them ***for your personal use*** in preparing your own speeches.

Speech Crafting

Main Message

Opening

1st Point

2nd Point

3rd Point

Close

Simple and to the point! Make notes in the appropriate boxes and then fine tune your thoughts and ideas as you move on to create your presentation.

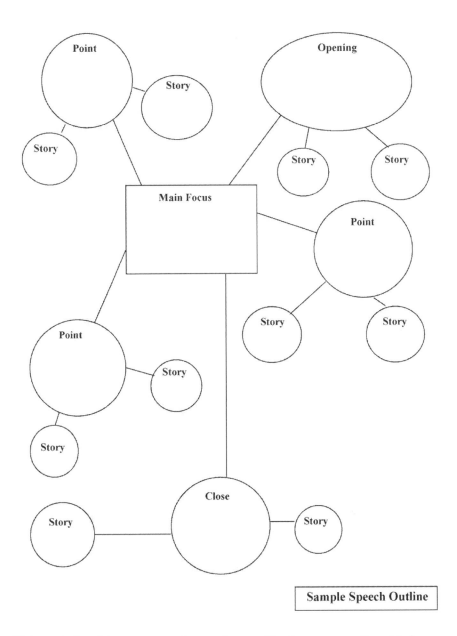

This style is a bit more creative and more like how most of us think.
Gather your points and organize them as you move ahead to create your presentation.

All about them...

Issue of some concern
(You're concerned ... I understand)

Point of view
(This is a different point of view ... of looking at your problem)

Support
(Here is how it will work for you ... the evidence)

Resolution (plan, proposal, idea)
(Here is the idea ... with benefits for you)

Next Step
(Here is your next step...)

Successful speakers keep their focus on the audience

Principles made personal yield powerful results - Ideas At Work!

Interpersonal communication

"It's important to talk to people in their own language. If you do it well, they'll say, 'He said exactly what I was thinking.' And when they begin to respect you; they'll follow you to the death." Lee Iacocca

Words are powerful, so choose them with great care. Keep in mind, the 500 most *commonly used* business words in the English language have over 14,000 definitions based on their usage and context.

Choose them *wisely* to best communicate the message you want to convey. Say it in their language, not yours. It works! Communication comes from the Latin root word *'commune,'* which loosely translated means *'held in common.'*

I worked with an interpreter (not a translator) when speaking in Vladivostok, Far Eastern Russia. She was a marvelous lady who taught at one of the universities. I noticed she would often take longer to share my thoughts in Russian than I did in English. I asked her why. She told me she wanted to make sure the audience understood my references so she added some informative bits to make it work better for all of us. And, she was funny so the audience laughed in most of the right places. This was one of my highlights for 2010. We're working to plan another visit for 2013.

To effectively communicate, we have to go the extra mile to ensure those we are talking with understand what we are saying, as well as we do. It is not just sending a message – it is creating a shared meaning and mutual understanding – quickly, clearly, and concisely. We must also be an *active* listener to ensure we draw out and understand what they are attempting to communicate to us.

This is a foundation for building a workable, lasting relationship – in work or in your personal life. When you establish such a relationship, **I'd suggest focusing on these areas:**

- **Be open**
- **Recognize**
- **Accept**
- **Appreciate other viewpoints**

This is the secret to effective communication – being open and flexible. How we listen and respond will dramatically impact our ability to understand and communicate.

Phrases that fire them up:
I like that; I'm glad you brought that up; That is great! We can do that; I agree; Yes, I think you might be onto something; Great work!; We can do something with that idea; Tell me more?; That is interesting, could you explain?

Phrases that dampen them:
Be practical; You haven't considered; The problem with that is…; I don't see how that can work; No way, that will work; If I had been doing it…; We don't have the time or money; Let me tell you…; I'm not interested, now get back to work.

"The real art of conversation is not only to say the right thing in the right place, but to leave unsaid the wrong thing at the tempting moment." **Dorothy Nevill**

To minimize the chance of being misunderstood, especially with so many definitions, take a moment and **paraphrase what is being said to you.**

- It helps you get on track – the same track – with the speaker.
- It helps you focus.
- It helps identify areas that need clearing up.
- It lets the other person know they are 'actually' being heard.
- It can help identify goals and common objectives – *'commune'*

Here are some examples of paraphrasing:

- Are you saying?
- If I heard you correctly?
- Am I understanding that you?
- Let me see if I understood you correctly?

Effective communication, as an active listener, is based on:

- Looking at the person
- Being an active, involved listener
- Asking questions
- Searching for common ground

- Being in the present – being present! *(Two words – two meanings!)*
- Not being stuck in the past or in history
- Focusing on ideas, concepts – not just the words
- Willing to deal with the issues, not the personalities
- Being positive and remaining open and flexible in your thinking.

"Communication does not begin with being understood, but with understanding others," W. Steven Brown

Did you know?

- At age one, the average child has a vocabulary of three words
- At fifteen months – nineteen words
- At two years of age – a working knowledge of 272 words
- Age three – big jump to 896 words
- Age four – 1,540 words
- Age five – 2072 words
- Age six – communication with 2,562 words

Ever wonder how many words we have each added to our list since we entered grade one? Have you consciously added to your vocabulary as tools to allow you to create more vivid word pictures?

Words are tools that help paint a mental picture. How many colors have you created in your palate to be able to paint word pictures more creatively?

"Give yourself an even greater challenge than the one you are trying to master and you will develop the powers necessary to overcome the original difficulty."
William J. Bennett - *The Book of Virtues*

Good stories = better speeches

Some of the world's greatest speakers are also great story tellers. Interesting observation, isn't it?

- My long-time friend and mentor, **Peter Legge** has gained international respect from his peers for his ability to weave a powerful, engaging story on the platform. Peter is amazing to experience, on and off stage.

- My friend, **Patricia Fripp** has the unique ability to add drama and a touch of Hollywood to make her stories memorable. She is in high demand as a speech coach primarily for this expertise.

There are too many more to mention here. I would worry I would forget some of the amazingly talented people I've grown to love and respect. If you would become a great speaker, you need to deal effectively with storytelling.

First of all, decide why you want to include or feature relevant stories in your presentation.

- Would they *actually* help you?
- What do you want to accomplish and *will stories add* to that objective?
- Which stories *reinforce* what you are trying to convey in your message?

Why do stories work?

- People like stories
- People pay attention
- People remember them
- Stories can stimulate *both sides* of the brain
- They can add humor
- Stories can be used as a motivational tool

If a picture is worth a 1000 words; at times a properly placed and performed story is worth 10,000 words in the minds of your audience.

Keep in mind the three basic STORY components:

- **The Premise**
- **The Problem**
- **The Payoff**

Each story has its own special use, placement, and characteristics. Learn to apply them where they are best suited to reinforce your message and help your audiences understand and retain your points.

One of the most impactful techniques I've acquired from several coaches and professional speakers is:

"Experience the story — don't just tell the story!"

It is important to help the audience *receive* your story on all three levels: visually, audibly, and, at times in a kinesthetic manner. Being ***in-the-moment*** helps form realistic mental images and anchor them in the minds of your audience.

There are 8 essential steps in a typical story development:

1. **Set the scene**
2. **Introduce the story's characters**
3. **Begin the journey**
4. **Encounter the obstacle, opportunity, or challenge**
5. **Overcome the obstacle, challenge, or engage the opportunity**
6. **Resolve the story**
7. **Make your point**
8. **Ask the question**

Understanding and applying the proper sequence in building a story will help you successfully re-create it in the minds of your audiences.

Two other techniques:

- Foreshadowing
- Flash backs

You might be familiar with these two as they are used in many applications: songs, movies, and books to mention a few.

Foreshadowing sets the audience up for something that will appear or be brought to the fore-front later in the speech.

Flash backs are a great way to take your audience back to an earlier time in the history or development of your story.

Using your own stories is a recipe for success on the platform.

- **Learning how to structure.**
- **Selecting the right story for the right moment or audience.**
- **Strategically placing stories for maximum impact.**
- **Adding a bit of drama or Hollywood pizzazz to help your audiences see the scene you are experiencing.**

Using stories effectively will do wonders for your success on the platform, on the sales floor, and in the boardroom.

The key ingredient to an effective speech is to have a unifying theme throughout.

These topics can help you structure or form interesting speeches that will keep the audience's attention.

1. **The importance of setting goals – dream big**
2. **Taking responsibility for your actions – personal leadership**
3. **Using mistakes to build a bright future – leveraged lessons**
4. **Finding inspiration in the world around you – observe**
5. **Never giving up on a dream – persevere and win**
6. **Creating a personal 'Code' to live by – integrity**
7. **The golden rule (Do Unto Others) – lead by example**
8. **Never forgetting your roots – keeping it real**
9. **Focusing on the important things in life – path to success**
10. **Setting high expectations – strive to grow**

Learning from the masters – a life-long lesson

I've been inspired by some great speakers over the years and share a few recollections and lessons from that inspiration. In 1972 I watched veteran entertainer **Art Linkletter** mesmerize his audience while I waited backstage for **Dr. Vincent Peale** to go on at the Jubilee Auditorium in Calgary, Alberta.

Off stage Dr. Peale sounded and acted like a typical grandpa. Visualize a 65 plus year old man, walking *slowly* on stage to thunderous applause, after being introduced by MC Don Hudson. I wondered how he would do.

He was inspirational! For nearly an hour he *captivated* that audience with the power of his 'enthusiasm' and the power of that gravelly, vibrant voice. Story after story about what we could do with our lives if we *believed;* really *believed*.

I was inspired… and a strange thought entered my mind…*"I would love to be able to do what he was doing!"* Well, some 22 years later, I followed him down this speaking path!

Show your passion – it moves people!

In 1992 I sat down for the first time with my now, long-time friend **Dr. Peter Legge, CSP**, **CPAE**, **HoF.** Peter was then only known to me as *the son* of my friend Bernie Legge.

I'd seen Peter speak and asked him for help with my Toastmasters Clubs when I was an Area Governor. I felt if they could see a *great* speaker, they might '*sense*' what they could gain from applying their skills. It might get them inspired. He spoke and inspired they got.

I asked Peter, "W*hat is the secret to being a great speaker?*" Peter told me the secret was *"…in telling your own stories"*. He shared that when he started he didn't think that anyone wanted to hear his stories, but found when he started sharing them his audience connection and his career vastly improved. I would say so!

Tell your own stories!

I shared my dream of becoming a professional speaker with a man I had met when he spoke along with best-selling author Og Mandino. He had invited me to call if I was ever in his neck of the world. Sitting in a fish and chips shop in Adelaide, Australia I listened as **Peter J. Daniels** challenged me to dream big – that my dreams were too small. He told me I needed to challenge myself to set and reach larger goals in my speaking career; that I would need bigger dreams to keep me focused and engaged to endure the risks, detours, and challenges I would encounter along the path I had chosen. He was right!

Take risks if you want results.

While sitting next to **Patricia Fripp, CSP, CPAE** during a NSA Platform Skills lab, I watched her madly writing notes as each presenter shared their ideas. I was amazed at how smart she was in writing down some of the same things I was. ☺ I learned that one of the reasons the great ones are great – they never stop learning, experimenting, or sharing. Thanks Fripp! Fripp challenged me to start sharing my *"Typhoon enroute to Japan"* story, as even though to me it was old, it would be fresh and exciting to my audiences. Was she right!

Use powerful words to explode the mental images of your stories.

Jim and **Naomi Rhode, CSP's** made a special trip to visit to our Vancouver, BC CAPS Chapter when I was President. Naomi skillfully wove stories from personal experience and observation into her session. I watched as my colleagues fell under her spell. Later, Jim talked about the importance of taking care of the business of speaking. I remember the first time I met Naomi. She came over to me after I'd spoken at CAMP-NSA, leaned into my ear and told me she loved what I said, and that *'I was a great speaker.'* I was both humbled and inspired by her *gracious* words.

Connect from the heart and share the little things. They matter!

There are many more speakers to whom I owe my inspiration, encouragement, and thanks. I've been inspired by many speakers within Toastmasters as well as the professional arena.

If you want to become a great speaker – hang out with great people and ask questions. You'll be amazed at what they are willing to teach you. Every month CAPS, NSA, GSF, and Toastmasters have meetings around the world. You have that opportunity. **Don't miss it!**

Presenting with passion and power

This is another exercise used with my students and executives. This one is geared to encourage them to speak with conviction about a subject they are passionate about. Again, the purpose is not to over think, but to speak and allow your passion to help your presentation.

Objectives of this exercise:
- To continue working on any nervousness you still have in speaking in front of an audience.
- To share with your audience your honest conviction, sincerity, and earnestness on a subject that is of great importance or concern to you.
- To project and apply your passion in being able to be a more powerful speaker.

Suggested presentation time: 2-3 minutes

For this exercise I'd suggest picking a topic that really concerns you, one on which you are passionate about; its defense, demise, or cause.

Be natural, yet forceful! Your major purpose is to convey your true and honest feelings to an audience. A combination of strong feeling and thought should allow you to give a true expression of your personality. Your goal is to share your focus with your audience and make them understand; and possibly join you in support of this enthusiastic point of view you express.

This project focus was chosen for a specific reason and was designed to help you succeed. **If something is important to you, it will reflect in your speech.** It will be easier for you to speak about something you deeply care about than to deliver a scripted or lackluster speech on a less important or assigned topic. You will gain confidence and confidence only when you are actually doing this in front of other people.

Awaken your audience with your introduction. Capture their attention. Make them sit up and want to listen to you. Interest them in your choice of subjects. Demonstrate your chosen topic's relevance and timeliness to them.

Identify the source of your concern and show how the problem or challenge can be solved during the body of your presentation. Bring your audiences' understanding and sympathy to your side, hopefully in support of you and your convictions.

A few general tips:

- **Be enthusiastic and positive** in your approach. This is a more effective way, even when dealing with a tough challenge or hostile audience.

- **Try it without notes**. You are telling your listeners what you really believe, rather than reading a script. Remember the 'hand' illustration. Since this is something you are passionate about it would lend itself to being delivered without notes.

- If you need notes, use cards where each point is illustrated by a simple phrase.

- If you're really ambitious, use large cards, graphs, charts, or power point slides to illustrate each main idea. Refer to these visual aids only as necessary.

- **Focus your 'nervous' energy** on the communication of your conviction, sincerity, and belief in the subject that you are presenting.

- Wind up with a **strong note of appeal or call to action** for your audience. Challenge them to do something 'GREAT' with what you've just told them. Remember the lesson from the Abraham Lincoln story.

- Assume you've won over your audience and challenge them to act on your message.

Take time to thoroughly rehearse this presentation. Try several different approaches and refine it as you go through each rehearsal. Enjoy the adventure!

Becoming effective and comfortable in front of an audience is attainable and cumulative – it takes time, practice, more practice, and persistence.

Applying the 3 R's in building
a good relationship with your audience

Remember the very old adage about the basics of learning, as it applied to schoolin' – the 3 R's, which were: **R**eading, w-**R**iting and a-**R**ithmetic! I would like to draw on a different set of 3 R's in my desire to assist you in successfully building a solid, impactful relationship with your audiences.

- A relationship that will allow you to more effectively deliver your message with impact and staying power.
- A relationship that will extend the trust you earn with them and continue to earn, as you deliver your message, set forth your case, and challenge them to act on what you've given them.

Let's explore 3 R's that can help you achieve this worthy goal.

Real
Is the message you seek to deliver real? Is it based on truth, grounded in reality, and filtered through the reality of your life and your experience? If so, you have a solid foundation on which to successfully build your relationship and to move your audience to actively respond to your challenge.

- Real does not mean you can't use creative license to make your stories live, to make them more vivid and memorable – but they must be based on truth to strike a chord in the lives of your audiences. **If they don't believe them – they won't believe you!**
- Real is how you convey your message, how you present yourself and how you connect. Who are you? Is your audience seeing the 'real' you? Faking it is a prelude to failure!

Hint: You don't always have to be the hero of your own stories. It is ok to share stories where you didn't win, or had to learn a serious lesson. Some of the most effective relationships I have had with audiences were built on honest discussion of the lessons learned from messing up. Given time to reflect and age a bit, our 'mess' can become a 'mess-age' of hope, encouragement, and empowerment. Isn't that what we want to accomplish as speakers?

Have the courage to be yourself and share you with your audiences – it will move them! **Real people learn and leverage from their lessons in life!**

Relevant
Is what you seek to share relevant to the audience's needs, experiences, relationships, or desires? How do you know? Have you invested the time to find out? This is where doing your homework works.

The more you know about your audience, the better chance you have of choosing the stories, word pictures, experiences, thoughts, and ideas that will relate to them. Building relevance takes time and diligence on our part – but if we truly desire to reach our audiences, it is our responsibility.

People relate to you when you share points that are relevant and real in their lives and experience. We seek a connection that will allow us to move them to action, not simply file away our words as more 'information'.

I repeat: This is where your homework or audience research pays off. Knowing them, what is it you can share from your experience, expertise, or research that would be the most beneficial? Then, work to weave that into your presentation.

Our goal is to build a bridge to shared learning and this bridge is anchored by ensuring what we share is relevant on both ends.

Relevance builds relationships.

Religion (Reaching out)
Now here I bet some of you are saying, *"OK, where did he get this from?"* Or, *"I don't get it – religion?"* But I do have a purpose here – stay with me. When I was attempting to sleep and was pondering this section, searching for a 3rd R, 'religion' came to mind. I immediately thought, *"No way – how does that apply?"*

I took a closer look to find the verse that had come to mind from a distant sermon, heard, filed, and seemingly forgotten. In the book of James he writes, *'**Religion** that God our father accepts as pure and faultless is this: **to look after orphans and widows in their distress…**'* James 1:27 NIV

He was taking about being a 'doer' of the word and not just a 'hearer' of the word – that 'real religion' was hands on, impacting, and helping people in their daily lives and struggles, not just words. Didn't Jesus model that?

The next morning, I suddenly saw the gem in the message he was conveying and understood how we can apply it in our desire to serve and challenge our audiences. I'm not talking about a spiritual connection, but a more person-to-person one.

To be effective, our message must be 'grounded' in a call to action for our audiences and built on our true desire to serve; to visit them in their affliction, confusion, or pain and to help them do something about it.

To that extent, when we put ourselves on the line and reach out to our audiences, we will see them respond and react to what we say. If we want to reach them, teach them, and move them to act on what we share, we need to visit them where they are (figuratively or metaphorically at least). They will respond to our efforts and give what we share more relevance when we do.

Religion in its purer sense is 'reaching out' in helping people and building a relationship to that end.

I remember saying to someone early on in this last recession, *"When things are tough, people need help and they need hope. That is just what I bring!"*

As speakers, we are at our best when this is where we are coming from when we deliver our message. When we seek to reach out to our audiences we can lift their sights and their spirits.

As I tell emerging speakers, consider there is at least one person in your audience who desperately needs to hear what you have to say. Our effectiveness as speakers is built on establishing relationships with those in our audiences.

Being real, working to establish 'relevance' and reaching out will go a long way to build solid foundation for your success on the platform, on the sales floor, and even in the boardroom!

Your voice as a powerful communication tool!

Your voice can be the most powerful tool in your communications by conveying information, meaning, emotion, and enthusiasm for your subject. It can also work against you, to make it hard for your audience to grasp what you are trying to say.

Early in my speaking journey I was taught that there are five basic characteristics of a good speaking voice.

1. A **pleasant tone**, which can convey a sense of warmth and friendliness.
2. A **vitality**, which lends the impression of force, strength, and conviction.
3. A **natural sound** that reflects and echoes your sincerity and true personality.
4. Portrays various **shades of meaning** to minimize monotony or lack of emotion.
5. **Easily heard:** learn and apply proper volume, projection, and **ar-tic-u-lation.**

Over the years I have sought coaching to help me develop my voice range and my projection. So, I am learning how to better use my voice as a tool or instrument and in that to be more effective in using it to its fullest potential.

The objective of a good speaking voice is to find, develop, and maintain a balance between the extremes of volume, pitch, and rate, while seeking to find and deliver a pleasing sound quality. It sounds hard, but it simply requires awareness and application of some basic principles. Perhaps a little coaching wouldn't hurt either. ☺

- **Volume**: can be varied to add emphasis or dramatic impact. Make sure everyone can hear you. Don't overpower your audience.

Early in my speaking career I encountered a situation where my soft-spoken style worked against me. I was speaking in San Diego to an overflow group of about 350 people in a long three-section room. The air conditioning in the center portion was very loud, which meant that when I went low to emphasize a point, that group couldn't hear me. This caused them to miss a good part of the message I was trying to convey.

Now, I know better to be aware and equipped to project, to ensure everyone can hear me. At the time I was a bit green and thought they could hear me with a sound system.

*I asked one of my coaches **John Howard** (now deceased), in Salt Lake City about it and he coached me. He even had me singing to work on it. As well, he referred me to one of his associates. She picked me up and we drove out into the desert foothills. We stopped and climbed this little hill in the 108-degree sun. About 300 yards up the hill; she stopped and motioned me to go on for another 100 yards. Once I was there she proceeded to have me give my speech so she could hear it. I learned a valuable lesson concerning projection without having to yell. Thanks **Billy Jones**, I owe you one.*

- **Pitch.** Can be varied to convey emotion and conviction. Avoid a too high pitch. This can suggest immaturity and excitability or reveal your nervousness. All of these take away from your strength and credibility as a presenter. Make a conscious effort to be *conversational* in your speaking. Focus on making it easy for your audience to hear and listen to you.
- **Rate.** Maintain a rate of 125-160 words per minute, which seems to be the most effective speaking rate. Vary your rate during your presentation to create emphasis and reflect mood changes. Slow down when you want the audience to listen carefully or emphasize an important point. Speed up to convey urgency or excitement in the moment.
- **Quality.** Relax your throat while you speak for increased vocal quality. Do a warm up before you begin to speak to allow your throat and muscles to prepare to deliver their best for you. *(I sometimes do it in the washroom before I am scheduled to speak.)* Think in terms of friendliness, confidence, and a desire to communicate clearly with your audience.
- **Tone.** Work to mold your tone; friendly and pleasant, not harsh and monotonous. Your audience will appreciate it and stay tuned to hear what you are saying.
- **Vitality.** Work on making your voice forceful and expressive when appropriate in your presentation and consistent with what you really feel. My fellow CAPS member Betty Cooper taught me to work on this area to add more vim to my vigor and make my stories sing with excitement.
- **Ar-tic-u-lation.** If they don't hear you clearly, you message will be lost. Work to be clear and distinct. Don't drop the hard letters like '*g*' at the end of words. Learn and apply the proper pronunciations for words.

Don't let your message be misunderstood just because your words are misunderstood.

In business, we have about 500 more commonly used English words with close to 5000 connotations. The wide range of connotations depends on how they are used and pronounced. Be clear, let us hear and understand you!

A few more comments…

- Practice using **warm up exercises** to give your voice its optimum range and to give your audience the best message possible.
- Make sure you **drink lots of water** – room temperature water with *no ice* before you speak. Don't be afraid to have water close at hand or to stop and take a sip from time to time while speaking. It's also a nice way to take a break and collect your thoughts. ☺
- A slice of lemon can be added to the water. Drinking ice water can be tough on your throat, as it tends to shrink or cause your muscles to contract. Remember the last time you had a sprain and had an ice pack. Don't do that to your throat, especially at a time when it is already under stress.
- Take a moment to **breathe and ground yourself** prior to speaking, especially if you've had a bit of a walk or gone up steps to a platform. This will give your voice a chance to adjust and be normal in a 'nervous' situation.
- Breathing is the most important point I can stress in being a good speaker. **Breathe from your diaphragm,** deeply and fully. Vocal sounds are made when air passes across your larynx. If you aren't breathing properly, your ability to project naturally is diminished.
- **Check out the room and sound system** before you speak. Try speaking in the spot where you'll be presenting to allow yourself to become acclimatized to the environment and to reduce your nervousness. Have the soundman adjust for your range from soft to the highest volume so you'll be comfortable and still be heard.
- **Don't smoke or drink coffee** or caffeine based products before you speak. The caffeine can act as a diuretic, putting pressure on your bladder when you really don't need it. Smoking will add hoarseness to your voice and minimize the fluid in your mouth. This can minimize your ability to fully speak and project warmth and friendliness.

Remember your voice box is a muscle. It works better when warmed up and taken care of prior to speaking.

Cowboys and communication

A cowboy gets up every day and knows he has a job to do... to get a herd of independently thinking cows across the prairies to a siding, where they will be shipped to market. He gains satisfaction from doing his job well and will continue to do so today and tomorrow and the day after that... because he is, a cowboy! Along the way he will battle unforgiving elements, sickness, boredom, balking cows, demanding terrain, and loneliness.

In our search as professional speakers, or to become effective communicators, we too will encounter numerous challenges... challenges that when overcome, will become the very foundations for our continuing success!

A cowboy doesn't think anything special about his skills and talents in roping, cutting, riding, or throwing... he just uses them as part of his daily tools in doing his job. Similarly with our communication skills, we need to take them into our daily lives and workplace to become truly proficient and effective in their use. Our audiences deserve our best! This is the essence of true professionalism! This is the secret behind Toastmasters International, NSA, CAPS, and the GSF in helping us to reach our goals and our audiences.

A cowboy doesn't whine when he comes to a detour or problem. He doesn't cry when his horse throws him. He gingerly picks himself up, dusts himself off, and gets back on again. When he comes to a dry hole, he simply mounts his horse and rides on in search of a well to water himself and his livestock.

Neither should we whine when we go through a dry spell...a relationship that doesn't work, a business that doesn't perform, or a speech that doesn't quite come off as well as we'd planned. We can, like the cowboy, simply pick ourselves up, refocus our energies, and move on in search of our future success!

A cowboy is the quintessential role model of the entrepreneurial communicator, in choosing his words carefully, planning and executing his actions wisely, and persistently focusing his energies on the job at hand. He listens slowly to hear the hidden meaning and then acts with confidence. We can learn well from this role model and can apply these same traits and dedications to our own success as speakers and communicators. Our audiences deserve our best!

Bob 'Idea Man' Hooey, *CKDE, DTM, Accredited Speaker*

101

Affirmations & visualization
The POWER of positive self-talk

Medal winning Olympic athletes, actors, writers, creative people, and, yes, even successful public and professional speakers have learned **the power of self-talk through affirmations** and the applied use of visualization techniques. These tools help them to **see** themselves performing at their best or presenting in a positive manner and enjoy the sense of accomplishment in advance.

Visualization is simple. ***Take a moment and imagine yourself*** *walking confidently to the front of the room, enjoying thunderous applause as you are introduced. Imagine walking up the stairs to the stage and shaking hands with your MC. Then imagine turning, taking a moment to make eye contact with the audience, as you ground yourself and take a few deep breaths. You smile and the audience smiles back at you! You feel accepted and confident! You visibly see and feel their support and encouragement. You begin your presentation with a strong clear voice and sense the excitement flowing through the crowd as your opening captivates their attention.*

As you continue to speak, you experience them laughing with you. Your heart soars with excitement. You skillfully lead them through the points you've outlined and you can see them ***'getting your message!'*** *You lead up to a powerful conclusion and end with a call to action that brings them to their feet clapping and cheering. You bask in the warmth of their appreciation and smile at them. As you return to your seat,* **you realize you never even had to look at your notes. You did great!**

Visualization allows your mind to experience the event before you perform it. The amazing thing is it can be so vivid, that when you actually get up to present you are more relaxed, because you've already done it.

It works very well, as I found out when I was preparing for each of my three performances in the accredited speaker program. I did this prior to leaving for the Toastmasters International conferences in San Diego, St. Louis, and finally Palm Desert. I also checked out the room where I would be presenting and did a quick run through of my presentation in the room. Finally, when I had a chance, I practiced walking across the main stage to receive my plaque as a professional level Accredited Speaker (way back in 1995).

In August 1998, on a hot sunny day, I walked across that stage in Palm Desert, CA to receive my award following the World Championships. I wondrously experienced, for real, the emotions I had earlier imagined, to the thunderous roar of applause, whistles, and cheers of over 2000 Toastmasters from around the world. **I had been there before – in my imagination THREE years earlier.**

Visualization is the secret to seeing and achieving your goals as a successful speaker. How do you keep yourself positive as you journey toward your goal? **Positive self-talk and affirmations** will work wonders to keep you focused and on track to your success.

Affirmations work by '**speaking the truth, as you would see it**' to your mind and your heart. To be effective affirmations must possess these three criteria.

- They must be **positive**!
- They must be in the **present tense** (today).
- And, they must be **personal**.

Here are some of the ones I've used over the years. Create your own, make them yours, and use them, as needed, on a **daily basis** for best results. I've used them individually or as groups. Create what works for you.

Having some instrumental music playing in the background helps me relax and enhances the experience. Try this for yourself when things are quiet and you won't be disturbed.

- My breathing is relaxed and effortless
- My heartbeat is slow and regular
- My muscles are relaxed and warm
- I feel at peace… I am at peace
- I am aware that I am a unique and special person
- Now is the best time to be alive… I am glad I am alive!
- I give the best of myself in everything I undertake!
- I keep the commitments I make
- I earn the respect of others
- I have a sense of adventure
- I have a sense of excitement!

- I am enjoying my work and the success I've earned
- I see new opportunities each day
- I am gentle… I demonstrate my caring for others
- I take time to play like a child… I enjoy my life
- I am strong… I am a winner!!!
- Today is the best day of my life… so far
- I thank GOD for His many gifts to me
- I encourage and support others in achieving their goals
- I am confident in my abilities and skills!
- I inspire confidence from my audiences!
- I grow friendships… I am a true friend
- I look for new ways to give value to my audiences
- I grow relationships with people I'd like to spend time with and learn from
- I offer a service that actually improves the quality of other's lives, to increase their wealth, well-being, and happiness
- I remember my presentation without pause or need of notes
- I know my subject and have selected that which is most valuable to share
- I am prepared, practiced, and polished for my presentation today!!!
- I will give each presentation as though it were my last
- I am excited about the opportunity to share my Ideas At Work!
- I will live my life today as though it was my last
- I will laugh and share my love with each person I meet

Try these on for size; change them or add to this list as you discover what is truly important for you. **Positive self-talk works.**

Listen to your heart! Then share your words with passion and power!

 *"There are always three speeches, for every one you actually gave. The one you practiced, the one you gave, and the one you wish you gave."*
Dale Carnegie

104

My Presentation Notes:

On the road... again!

Time and time I hear the amazement and sometimes envy in people's voices when they comment on what I do for a living – travel the world sharing my **Ideas At Work!** and encouraging people to live life as an adventure. I love what I do, but it is, at times, tough mentally and physically. Being what they call a 'road warrior' takes its toll. Ask anyone who travels regularly for work and they'll agree on the costs.

 Newer speakers and audience members say things like, ***"Must be nice to fly all over the world!"*** Or, ***"You get to stay in nice hotels!"*** Or, ***"You get to eat out in nice restaurants too!"*** In part, these comments are very true. In the interest of full disclosure, some of this wears thin at times. The *novelty* wore off about a dozen years ago. **I still, very much, love what I do. I am more aware of the cost of being on the road;** a cost to my health, my comfort, and sometimes to relationships. This is one of the reasons I savor opportunities to speak closer to home.

Pictured here (above left) heading out, again; packed, prepared, and full of potential.

In any role there are trade-offs. I accept that and advise newer speakers that it is not **all** fun and games. It can, at times, be arduous!

Sitting in airports waiting for a delayed flight due to mechanical or weather challenges is tiring, even fatiguing. Sitting in a seat for 8-18 hours flight time can beat you down. Fast food eaten on the fly, if you have time, doesn't help your digestion. Running through airports to catch a flight, because your last one came in late, is not real exercise.

Eating alone, in a strange new place is never fun. Sleeping in a strange bed without the woman you love is boring at best. Sleeping a strange bed itself is a challenge for me. It often takes me a day or two to acclimatize. Sadly, I may not be there more than one night.

On the positive side, meeting new people, enjoying new adventures and seeing parts of the globe only seen on TV are amazing. Being well paid to do so and having your expenses covered is very nice. I have the opportunity to explore different cultures and see first-hand the similarities we share. I am able to share my ideas and exchange lessons with my new friends. I have new friends around the world and been able to travel to 35 countries on 4 continents, so far. I expect to visit many more in the years to come. Irene's retirement will allow her to come on some of the adventures.

This picture (above right) was taken along the banks of the Seine in Paris where Irene met me on my way back from speaking in Mumbai, India. Once in a while she gets to come along or meet me enroute. I look forward to having her join me on many new adventures in the future.

So, if I was absolutely honest, I would say this role I have chosen has its drawbacks and its challenges. It is hard on me physically more so than mentally. It challenges me to see beyond the current discomfort to the future satisfaction. **Being a travelling professional speaker is the hardest career you'll ever love.**

Enjoy the journey.

Here (above) Irene and I enjoy a reflective moment in front of one of the most famous smiles in the world. We smiled in response.

"What lies behind us and what lies before us are tiny matters compared to what lies within us."
Oliver Wendell Holmes

The Spirit of CAPS award

Have you ever been totally surprised at something? Surprised that you had done something that people actually noticed? So surprised you were almost speechless? Me too!

The trip to Toronto for our 2011 CAPS convention started with a hectic rush to make airline connections to arrive just in time to help my friend Wayne Lee with the CAPS Foundation fundraising event we'd worked on for about 6 months. It was a gratifying success, raising **$35,083** over the evening. This was a great highlight for the year for me, for my fellow CAPS Foundation Trustees, and for the work everyone put into this evening.

Then, at the end of the awards banquet the next evening, **2011 CAPS President Ravi Tangri** came on stage to present **The Spirit of CAPS,** which is the highest award we present within the Canadian Association of Professional Speakers. We have given it previously to only 10 speakers in our 15 year history

"The Spirit of CAPS may be awarded to one CAPS member each year who demonstrates the spirit of sharing, leading, and inspiring other professional speakers, trainers, and facilitators within the mission, vision, and values of CAPS. This member will have demonstrated the qualities of generosity, spirit, and professionalism over many years and reflected outstanding credit, respect, honor, and admiration in the Association."

When Ravi was introducing this year's recipient, he mentioned this person was the **1st Canadian to attend CAMP NSA.** I realized he was talking about me. I couldn't believe what I was hearing. I was both shocked and deeply touched at the same time.

As I wiped the tears from my eyes on the way to the stage to accept this amazing award, I wondered what I would say. From what people said, I simply shared this award with the hundreds of people who said 'yes' when I asked for help. Also, even though I was singled out for this honor, I did not achieve it alone. I had help!

Visit: **www.ideaman.net/SoC.htm** for more information on this award, my acceptance speech, and my fellow recipients.

We don't work for the honors and the recognition, but it sure is nice to find out someone noticed and appreciated our efforts. That, in itself, spurs us on to find other ways to serve. It does me!

Writing and rewriting this book is in itself a way to continue that service to helping others find their voice and hone their message.

Bob 'Idea Man' Hooey
2011 Spirit of CAPS Recipient
2012 CAPS Edmonton President

 *"The greater danger for most of us lies not in setting our aim too high and falling short; but in setting our aim too low, and achieving our mark."*
Michelangelo

Accredited Speaker Program

Over the past 14 years, many people have inquired about my Accredited Speaker Designation and how it came to be. As it played a critical part in my desire to become a professional speaker, I include this brief story of my journey for your information.

In November of 1993, 32 Toastmasters from around the world sent in audition tapes and applications for judging in the first level of the Toastmasters International prestigious professional level Accredited Speaker Program.

In February of 1994, *only five* were notified of acceptance and invited to speak at the Toastmasters International convention for second level judging. Of those five, three were Canadians. All three were from BC, from the same Toastmasters Club – the Advanced Speaker Klub. They were Margaret Hope, Judy Johnson, and myself.

How did this unique result happen?

It started back in 1992, when seven BC Toastmasters met to investigate the Toastmasters International Accredited Speaker program and continued to meet monthly for the next year and a bit. Each month we would meet, present, and evaluate our results. We worked as a team in all respects including creating a non-Toastmasters event where we each presented and recorded our presentations. We did that twice so we could choose the better of the two recordings. In November of 1993, Margaret Hope, Judy Johnson, and I felt ready to apply and sent in our audition tapes.

Margaret received her Accredited Speaker designation in San Diego in 1995, becoming the 41st speaker inducted into Toastmasters Hall of Fame for this award. Judy and I were not successful in our first attempt in San Diego. I spoke again the following year in St. Louis and was not successful. I took 1997 off as I had taken on the District Governor role for BC's 4500 Toastmasters. But I kept working on it to hone my skills. I moved into the realm of professional speaking taking my presentations to a new level. I helped found CAPS Vancouver in April of 1997 as a part of CAPS National across Canada.

The dream became a reality when I walked across a stage to the cheers of 2000-plus, fellow Toastmasters from around the world to be inducted into the Toastmasters hall of fame and received mine in Palm Desert in 1998; becoming the 48 Accredited Speaker in our history, and only the 5th Canadian to earn this designation.

To date (2012), there were only sixty-three people world-wide, who have made this walk of fame following the world championships. Only seven are Canadians.

Toastmasters initiated their professional level, Accredited Speakers program in 1981, some 30 years ago. **Visit: www.Toastmasters.org** for more information on the program and its Hall of Fame recipients.

I focused on this program early in my TM life, as my dream was to become a professional speaker. I remember when I got my Able Toastmaster (ATM); it came with a flyer for the Accredited Speaker Program which said in big letters, **"Are you good enough to be a PRO?"** I wrote on it, **'Not yet, but I will be!"** For two years it challenged me!

The real win in this program, wasn't the designation itself or the worldwide recognition, although that was very satisfying. **The *real win* for me was in the progression of my skills and entry into the world of professional speaking;** in being able to have people see, first hand, the value in what I brought to the training room or the platform and pay me accordingly.

The real win was in being better at sharing my messages for the benefit of my audiences around the world.

If you have a dream to become a professional trainer, facilitator, or keynoter, then perhaps you should investigate this program. For me the journey was well worth the effort.

111

Thanks for purchasing and reading
Speaking for Success

Each time I prepare to step on the stage; each time I sit down to write or in this case to re-write, I am challenged to ensure I deliver something that will be of use-it-now value to my reader.

- I ask myself, *"If I was reading this, what would I be looking for?"*
- As well as, *"Why is this relevant to me, today?"*

These two questions help to keep me focused and help me to remain clear on my objectives. They help to remind me to dig into my experiences, stories, examples, and research to provide solid information that will be of benefit and help my readers, when they apply it, succeed. That can be an exciting challenge!

I trust I have done that for you in this updated primer on more effective communication and presentation skills. **Speaking for Success** is my attempt to capture some of the lessons learned first-hand on stage and sharing the stage with many speaking masters and to share them with you.

I'd love to hear from you and read your success stories. If you would be so kind, please drop me a quick email at: **bob@ideaman.net**

Bob 'Idea Man' Hooey
2011 Spirit of CAPS recipient
www.ideaman.net
www.HaveMouthWillTravel.com
Pictured (left) in Mumbai, India

Connect with me on:
- **Facebook:** www.facebook.com/bob.hooey
- **LinkedIn:** www.linkedin.com/in/canadianideamanbobhooey
- **YouTube:** www.youtube.com/ideamanbob
- **Smashwords:** www.smashwords.com/profile/view/Hooey

About the author

Bob 'Idea Man' Hooey is a charismatic, confident leader, corporate trainer, inspiring facilitator, Emcee, prolific author, and motivational keynote speaker on creativity, sales success, business innovation, and enhancing team performance.

Using personal stories drawn from rich experience, he challenges his audiences to engage his **Ideas At Work! – to act on what they hear,** with clear, innovative building-blocks and field-proven success techniques to increase their effectiveness. Bob challenges them to hone specific 'success skills' critical to their personal and professional advancement.

Bob outlines real-life, results-based, innovative ideas personally drawn from 29 plus years of rich leadership experience in retail, sales, construction, small business, entrepreneurship, manufacturing, association, consulting, community service, and commercial management.

Bob's conversational, often humorous, professional, and sometimes-provocative style continues to inspire and challenge his audiences across North America. Bob's motivational, innovative, challenging, and practical **Ideas At Work!** have been successfully applied by thousands of sales leaders and professionals across the globe.

Bob is a frequent contributor to North American consumer, corporate, association, trade, and on-line publications on leadership, sales success, employee motivation and training; as well as creativity and innovative problem solving, priority and time management, and effective customer service. He is the inspirational author of 25 plus publications including print, e-books, and a Pocket Wisdom series. Visit: **www.SuccessPublications.ca** for more information.

Retired, award winning kitchen designer, Bob Hooey, CKD-Emeritus was one of only 75 Canadian designers to earn this prestigious certification by the National Kitchen and Bath Association.

In December 2000, Bob was given a special CAPS National Presidential award **"for his energetic contribution to the advancement of CAPS and his living example of the power of one"** in addition to being elected to the CAPS National Board. He has been recognized by the National Speakers Association for his leadership contributions.

Bob was a co-founder and past President of the CAPS Vancouver Chapter and currently serves as 2012 President of the CAPS Edmonton Chapter. He is a member of the NSA-Arizona Chapter and is active in the National Speakers Association, the Canadian Association of Professional Speakers, as well as the Global Speakers Federation.

In 1998, Toastmasters International recognized Bob **"for his professionalism and outstanding achievements in public speaking"**. That August in Palm Desert, California Bob became the 48th speaker in the world to be awarded this prestigious professional level honor as an Accredited Speaker. He has been inducted into their Hall of Fame on several other occasions for his leadership contributions.

Bob has been honored by the United Nations Association of BC (1993) and received the CANADA 125 award (1992) for his ongoing contributions to the community.

In 1998, Bob joined 3 other men to sail a 65 foot gaff rigged schooner from Honolulu, Hawaii to Kobe, Japan, barely surviving a 'baby' typhoon enroute.

In November 2011 Bob was awarded The Spirit of CAPS at their annual convention, becoming the 11th speaker to earn this prestigious award.

Bob loves to travel and his speaking and writing have allowed him to visit 35 countries so far. Perhaps your organization would like to bring Bob in to share a few ideas with your team. Visit: **www.HaveMouthWillTravel.com** for more information.

Bob's Publications

Bob is a prolific author who has been capturing and sharing his wisdom and experience in printed and electronic forms for the past twelve plus years. In addition to the following publications he has written for consumer, corporate, professional associations, trade, and on-line publications. He has been engaged to write and assist on publications by other writers and companies. His publications are listed to give you an idea of the scope and topics he writes about.

Leadership, Business, Sales, and Career Development Series

- I'm Already Running as Fast as I Can!
- Secrets of EFFECTIVE Customer Service
- Why Didn't I 'THINK' of That?
- **Speaking for Success!** (7th Edition updated for 2012)
- A Quest for Balance (SFS companion)
- Creating TIME to Sell, Lead, or Manage
- Thinking Beyond the FIRST Sale
- Create the Future
- A Legacy of Leadership
- CONFLICT - Dealing effectively with conflict
- Get to YES! - The subtle art of persuasion in negotiation (EPUB)
- For Immediate Release – The Personal Power of Public Relations
- Media Management - What to say if a reporter calls
- Winning in the Boardroom – Maximized meetings that get results THINK Before You Ink! (EPUB)
- Running to Win! (EPUB)
- Coaching for Optimal Results
- Success Skills for Leaders, Entrepreneurs and those Who Support Them

Bob's Mini-book series

- TALK, So People Will Listen
- The Courage to Lead!
- LEAD, So People Will Follow
- Creativity Counts!
- How to Generate More Sales
- Sales Success - Sampler and Companion
- Unleash your Business Potential
- My 'Next' Million Dollar Idea Book
- Learn to Listen
- Thanks Mom!
- Dad, You're Still My Hero

Bob's Pocket Wisdom Series

- Pocket Wisdom for Selling Professionals
- Pocket Wisdom for Speakers
- Pocket Wisdom for Innovators
- Pocket Wisdom for Leaders
- Pocket Wisdom for Business Builders
- Additional PW books are coming in 2012

Co-authored e-books

- Quantum Success – 3 volume series
- In The Company of Leaders
- Foundational Success

Visit: www.SuccessPublications.ca for more information on Bob's publications and other success resources.

"Speaking is simple when you focus on the audience and do your homework, before you open your mouth and heart."
Bob 'Idea Man' Hooey

A few thoughts on communication

Let thy speech be better than silence or be silent. *Dionysius*

Speech was made to open man to man, and not to hide him; to promote commerce, and not betray it. *David Lloyd*

The human brain is a wonderful thing. It operates from the moment you're born until the first time you get up to make a speech. *Howard Goshorn*

Speech is a mirror of the soul: as a man speaks, so is he. *Publilius Syrus*

In interpersonal communication, there must be an ongoing and perceived consistency between what you say and how you say it. *Janet Elsea*

The most important thing in communication is to hear what isn't being said. *Peter Drucker*

Communication does not begin with being understood, but with understanding others. *W. Steven Brown*

Good communication is as stimulating as black coffee and just as hard to sleep after. *Ann Morrow Lindbergh*

The right word may be effective, but no word was ever as effective as a rightly timed pause. *Mark Twain*

There may be no single thing more important in our efforts to achieve meaningful work and fulfilling relationships than to learn to practice the art of communication. *Max De Pree*

Wise men talk because they have something to say; fools, because they have to say nothing. *Plato*

To speak much is one thing, to speak well another. *Sophocles*

A man's character is revealed by speech. *Menander*

Feel free to investigate these organizations. Each has their specific focus and each has, at their core, a dedication to help people be more effective as presenters.

TMI - Toastmasters International:
www.Toastmasters.org
This is where I got my start and built most of the foundations for my entrance into the speaking business. I remain active in my local advanced club as I continue to learn and hone my skills.

NSA - National Speakers Association:
www.NSAspeaker.org
Before we started CAPS, four of us travelled down to Seattle every month to attend the NSA chapter to learn more about this new business we had become a part of. It was a long drive but worth the trip.

Canadian Association of Professional Speakers:
www.CanadianSpeakers.org
CAPS became a national organization in 1997 following the creation of what has become the Global Speakers Federation. I had the privilege of helping start the CAPS Vancouver Chapter which in itself helped to create our National organization.

Global Speakers Federation
www.globalspeakers.net
This is the umbrella organization of 12 national speaking organizations.

Alberta Speakers:
www.AlbertaSpeakers.com
This is a simple joint venture project we started 7 years ago with professional speakers from Alberta. We each contribute to support the website and buy print advertisements that promote the website.

What clients say about Bob 'Idea Man' Hooey

As I travel across North America, and more recently around the globe, sharing my **Ideas At Work!** I am fortunate to get feedback and comments from my audiences. These comments come from people who have been touched, challenged, or simply enjoyed themselves in one of my sessions. The leveraged lessons as contained in **Speaking for Success** have allowed me to gain this positive and professionally satisfying response. If you are willing to apply yourself and practice and polish you too can leave these kinds of impressions. **Enjoy the journey!**

"I still get comments from people about your presentation. **Only a few speakers have left an impression that lasts that long.** *You hit a spot with the tourism people."* Janet Bell, Yukon Economic Forums

"We greatly appreciate **the energy and effort you put into researching and adapting your keynote to make it more meaningful to our member councils.** *Early feedback from our delegates indicates that this year's convention was one of our most successful events yet, and we thank you for your contribution to this success."* Larry Goodhope, Executive Director Alberta Assoc. of Municipal Districts & Counties

"Thank you Bob; it is **always a pleasure to see a true professional at work.** *You have made the name "Speaker" stand out as a truism - someone who encourages people to examine their lives and make adjustments. The personal stories you shared with your audience made such a great impression on everyone.* **The comments indicated you hit people right where it is important - in their hearts.** *Each of those in your audience took away a new feeling of personal success and encouragement."* Sherry Knight, Dimension Eleven Human Resources and Communications

"Attention Training Providers: *I want to take this opportunity to let you know that Bob Hooey has utilized his talents, energy and considerable public speaking experience to provide communications clinics for our BC Works! clients. They have been very successful... reporting dramatically increased confidence and self-esteem!* **In addition to being a highly skilled facilitator, Bob has shown himself to be a great team player with a comfortable manner and a great sense of humor."** Vicki Austad, Manager, New Westminster Community Skills Centre

"Bob is one of those rare individuals who knows how to tackle obstacles in life to reach his dreams. He takes each as a learning experience and stretches for more. **His compassion and genuine interest in others, make him an exceptional coach**.*"* Cindy Kindret, Training Manager, Silk FM Radio

"Now that the **Active Minds session for Chapters** *has drawn to a close, I want to thank you for all you have done to help make the program such a success.* **Feedback** *from the store Managers, and directly from customers,* **was entirely enthusiastic.** *Their remarks and words of appreciation have made it obvious that everyone who participated in your courses benefited enormously from your intelligence and insights.* **Your energy, creativity, and ability to communicate effectively - especially with such a diverse audience and under conditions that are so noticeably less than ideal -make your efforts all the more impressive and praiseworthy.** *I know, as do all I work with at Chapters, just how indebted we are to you. My thanks are double-barreled...* **you have made it possible for me to provide a program that is of real value** *to the public - and you have made the task of organizing and implementing this program pure pleasure."* Suzy Okun, National Co-coordinator, Chapters Active Minds Series

"Without doubt, **I have gained immeasurable self-assurance***. Bob, your patience and your encouragement has been much appreciated.* **I strongly recommend your course to anyone looking for self-improvement and professional development***."* Jeannie Mura, Human Resources Chevron Canada

"I have found **Bob's attention to detail** *and his ability to fine tune his seminars to match the time frame and needs of the audience to be a valuable asset to our educational program."* Patsy Schell, Executive Director Surrey Chamber of Commerce

"I am pleased to recommend Bob 'Idea Man' Hooey to any organization looking for a charismatic, confident speaker and seminar leader. I have seen Bob in action on several occasions, and he is ALWAYS on! Bob has the ability to grab his audience's attention and keep it. Quite simply, **if Bob is involved - your program or seminar is guaranteed to succeed***."* Maurice Laving, Coordinator Training and Development, London Drugs

"Just a note to say thanks so much for running our recent seminar for employees on **strategic planning***. Everyone still talks about how much help it was to all of us. The wealth of information you gave us in the handbook was a great help also, and* **something we couldn't have done on our own***."* Chuck & Joan Guild, Uni-Pro Printing & Design, Burnaby, BC

"Great seeing you in Cancun and congratulations on a job well done. **The seminar was a great success! Your humorous and conversational style was a tremendous asset***. It is my sincere hope that we can be associated again at future seminars."* Donald MacPherson, Attorney At Law, Phoenix, Arizona

"What a great conference*. It was a great pleasure meeting with you at the Ritz Carlton, Cancun and I shall look forward to hopefully welcoming you and your family in Dublin, Ireland someday."* A. Paul Ryan, Petronva Corporation, Dublin, Ireland

"You are a wonderful speaker and did a **great job at drawing the audience in** *with you as you shared some of the stories about the women who made a difference in your personal and professional life."* Pavala Michaela Polcarova, Event Coordinator, The Special Women in Our Lives

Bob has coached and the Senior Executive members of the District 42 Toastmasters for several years, serving as a Trainer & Mentor at our annual experiential training event. In addition to sharing his knowledge and experience with the leaders in our organization, he has been very helpful & influential to me personally. Bob is worth every penny of your investment in his services... and then some! But let's not tell him that!! **Troy Wruck**, DTM, Past District 42 Governor, Toastmasters International

Bob delivers a value packed program based on 'what about you' and not 'what about Bob." Bob is a master of drawing the audience in as a full partner. Thanks Bob, I learn from you whenever I see you! **Jamie Hayward**, Oxford Properties

Bob 'Idea Man' Hooey is one of the best public speakers I know, and I have seen and heard many over the years. His style will educate, entertain, and inspire any audience. I very strongly recommend the 'Idea Man' for any organization that needs to hear a positive message, and wants that extra bit of help moving the ship in the right direction! **Paul Holmes,** President, Transitional Media Inc.

"You are a dynamic speaker and **you provided us with many ideas for making our businesses more successful** *with your presentation of "Unlock Your Business Potential." The comments we received from the meeting were very positive. Many especially found it useful to record some key points on the postcard and will look forward to receiving it prior to your next session."* Barb Nicholl, Woman's AM

11250167R00072

Made in the USA
Charleston, SC
10 February 2012